PREFACE

General Editor: JOHN PURKIS

'A description of what the *Preface Books* were intended to be was included in the first volume and has appeared unchanged at the front of every succeeding title: "A series of scholary and critical studies of major writers intended for those needing modern and authoritative guidance through the characteristic difficulties of their work to reach an intelligent understanding and enjoyment of it." This may seem modest enough but a moment's reflection will reveal what a considerable claim it actually is. It is much to the credit of Longman and to their (founding) editor Maurice Hussey and his authors that these words have come to seem no more than a plain statement of fact.'

NATE NEWS

Titles available in the series:

A portrait of Lawrence c. 1923 by the Danish painter Knud Merrild who was a neighbour of the Lawrences in New Mexico.

A PREFACE TO

D.H. LAWRENCE

GĀMINI SALGĀDO

Longman

An imprint of **Pearson Education**

Harlow, England · London · New York · Reading, Massachusetts · San Francisco
Toronto · Don Mills, Ontario · Sydney · Tokyo · Singapore · Hong Kong · Seoul
Taipei · Cape Town · Madrid · Mexico City · Amsterdam · Munich · Paris · Milan

GĀMINI SALGĀDO was formerly Professor of English at Exeter University. His work on Lawrence developed while reading for a doctorate at Nottingham, the novelist's own university. He has published a book on *Sons* and *Lovers* (Studies in English Literature, Arnold) and edited an anthology of criticism of it (Macmillan Casebooks). In addition he has published a number of editions and other studies of drama and prose literature, most recently *English Drama: A Critical Introduction* (Arnold).

Pearson Education Limited
Edinburgh Gate
Harlow
Essex CM20 2JE
England

and Associated Companies throughout the world

Visit us on the World Wide Web at:
www.pearsoneduc.com

First published 1982

ISBN 0 583 43766 0 PPR

British Library Cataloguing-in-Publication Data
A catalogue record for this book can be obtained from the British
Library.

Library of Congress Cataloging-in-Publication Data
A catalog record for this book can be obtained from the Library of
Congress.

10 9 8 7 6 5 4 3 2 1
04 03 02 01

Set in 10/11pt Baskerville MT
Produced by Pearson Education Asia Pte Ltd.,
Printed in Singapore

To my daughter Kumari

'For man, the vast marvel is to be alive. For man, as for flower, beast and bird, the supreme triumph is to be most vividly, most perfectly alive. Whatever the unborn and the dead may know, they cannot know the beauty, the marvel of being alive in the flesh. The dead may look after the afterwards. But the magnificent here and now of life in the flesh is ours, and ours alone, and ours only for a time. We ought to dance with rapture that we should be alive and in the flesh, and part of the living, incarnate cosmos. I am part of the sun as my eye is part of me. That I am part of the earth my feet know perfectly, and my blood is part of the sea. My soul knows that I am part of the human race, my soul is an organic part of the great human soul, as my spirit is part of my nation. In my own very self I am part of my family. There is nothing of me that is alone and absolute except my mind, and we shall find that the mind has no existence by itself, it is only the glitter of the sun on the surface of the waters.'

D. H. Lawrence, *Apocalypse*.

Author's note

Students and colleagues, past and present, and critics of Lawrence have shaped my own views in ways I can no longer clearly identify, if I ever could. I am grateful to them and also to Melba Chapman for her indefatigable energy and unfailing cheerfulness while she tidied an Augean manuscript into a presentable typescript. Fenella Mitchell helped with more than the proofs. Finally, I am especially fortunate to have had an editor with the patience, good humour and understanding of Maurice Hussey. No one but myself is to blame for whatever blemishes remain in the book.

G.S.

Contents

List of illustrations

Foreword

Richard Aldington, Lawrence's friend and biographer, believed that England owed the novelist a posthumous apology. No longer. If he had been criticized, censored and dismissed in his lifetime he now stands as the major imaginative novelist of early twentieth-century England and one who attained that eminence by the comprehensiveness of his human understanding and sympathy. It is probably of equal importance that, didactic as he was, he did not forfeit the virtue, so strongly cultivated by Dickens, George Eliot and Hardy, of wide comprehensibility and a steadily widening reading public.

As Gāmini Salgādo reminds us, all who knew Lawrence at all well felt the urge to place their record in print. Each one added a small portion to the story of the novelist's pilgrimage from the English midlands and across much of the globe. Aldous Huxley explained the attraction of his friend in that "he was everything so much more intensely and completely than ordinary men." In the first section of this *Preface* the life is recounted in satisfying depth, but it is when we are encouraged to link that biography with its intellectual and artistic roots (from p. 64) that Professor Salgādo's own deep understanding of Lawrence takes on its most completely sensitive and helpful form.

Chief among the many works studied in the second half of the book are inevitably *Sons and Lovers* and *The Rainbow*. Here the author asks the most interesting questions and provides answers controlled by an exacting respect for the text and an unfailing sense of what will help the reader to refine and articulate his own responses. All the analyses provided are full of clear, vivid, convincing and most frequently memorable critical writing. The flame from Lawrence's work is passed on with a vitality that must communicate itself to readers of all ages who want to be more perfect Lawrentians.

MAURICE HUSSEY, General Editor

Acknowledgements

We are grateful to the following for supplying photographs and for permission to reproduce them:
BBC Hulton Picture Library, page 139; British Library, page 20; David Garnett Estate, page 165; Saki Karavas Collection, Taos, New Mexico, page ii; cartoon by Sir David Low by permission of the Low Trustees and the *Evening Standard*, page 126; Mansell Collection, page 25; Edward Nehls, *D. H. Lawrence: A Composite Biography*, Volume II, University of Wisconsin Press, 1957, page 55 below (original photograph owned by Roy MacNicol); Nottinghamshire County Library, Local Studies Library, pages 10, 12, 16 (original photograph owned by Nottingham University Library), 21 (original photograph owned by H. G. Guns), 26 (original photograph in private collection), 28 (original photograph owned by Helen Corke), 31 (original photograph owned by C. Montague Weekley), 40 (original photograph owned by H. T. Moore), and 69; Nottingham University Library Manuscripts Department, pages 43 (Gerald Pollinger and estate of Frieda Lawrence), 61 (original photograph owned by Mrs. O. L. Hopkin), 63 (original photograph owned by George L. Lazarus), 143 (photograph by Edward Weston), 147 (original photograph owned by Frances Gair Wilkinson), 172 (photograph by Warren Roberts) and 174; Gāmini Salgādo, pages 55 above and 64; University of Texas at Austin, Humanities Research Department, pages 59 and 109.

The painting *An Idyll* by Maurice Greiffenhagen, which Lawrence copied several times, is reproduced on the cover by permission of the Walker Art Gallery, Liverpool.
For permission to adapt the following maps:
Boulton J. T. (editor), *The Letters of D. H. Lawrence* Volume I, Cambridge University Press, page 35; Nottingham University Library, pages 169 and 171.

Part One
The Writer and his Setting

Chronological table

	LAWRENCE'S LIFE	HISTORICAL EVENTS
1885	Born at Victoria Street, Eastwood Nottinghamshire, 11 September.	
1887	Lawrence family moves to a house overlooking the Breach, Eastwood ('The Bottoms' in *Sons and Lovers*)	
1890	Lawrence family move to Walker Street, Eastwood	
1892	At Beauvale Board School (till 1898).	Death of Tennyson.
1898	Wins scholarship to Nottingham High School (till 1901).	
1901	Works for three months as clerk at Haywoods surgical appliance factory. Dangerously ill with pneumonia. Death of Lawrence's brother Ernest. Meets Jessie Chambers.	Death of Queen Victoria.
1902	Family moves to Lynncroft Road, Eastwood. Pupil teacher at British School, Eastwood (till 1905).	
1904	On course for pupil teachers at Ilkeston. With fellow-teachers (including Jessie Chambers and Louise Burrows) forms an intellectual circle, the Pagans.	

1905	Writes his first poems.
1906	At Nottingham University College for a two-year teacher-training course (till 1908). Begins *The White Peacock*.
1907	Writes 'The White Stocking'. His first publication. 'A Prelude' (submitted for a short story competition under the name of Jessie Chambers) appears in the *Nottinghamshire Guardian*.
1908	Teacher at Davidson Road School, Croydon. Meets Helen Corke.
1909	Writes 'Odour of Chrysanthemums'. Poems published in *The English Review*, edited by Ford Madox Ford.
1910	Death of Lawrence's mother. Engaged to Louise Burrows. Completes *The White Peacock*, begins *The Trespasser* and *Sons and Lovers* (at first called *Paul Morel*).
1911	*The White Peacock* published. Writes 'Daughters of the Vicar'. Meets Edward Garnett. Second serious attack of pneumonia.
1912	Leaves Croydon. Meets Frieda Weekley and goes with her to Germany and Italy. *The Trespasser* published. *Sons and Lovers* finished. Breaks off

1906 — John Galsworthy's *The Man of Property* published. Liberals win General Election.

1908 — Arnold Bennett's *The Old Wives' Tale* published.

1909 — Death of Swinburne.

engagement to Louise
Burrows.

1913   Returns to England with
        Frieda. Breaks off relations
        with Jessie Chambers.
        Meets J. M. Murry and
        Katherine Mansfield. *Love
        Poems and Others* and *Sons and
        Lovers* published. Returns to
        Continent and begins work
        on *The Sisters* (later to
        become *The Rainbow* and
        Women in Love) and *The
        Lost Girl*.

1914   Back in England. Married   Outbreak of First World
        to Frieda 13 July. Meets   War, 4 August.
        Ottoline Morrell. *The
        Widowing of Mrs Holroyd* and
        The Prussian Officer
        published. Living at
        Chesham, Buckinghamshire.

1915   *The Rainbow* published and
        suppressed within weeks.
        Edits *The Signature* with
        Murry and Katherine
        Mansfield. Meets Aldous
        Huxley. Plans a lecture
        series with Bertrand Russell.
        Living at Pulborough,
        Sussex and London. Writes
        A Study of Thomas Hardy.

1916   Living in Cornwall. *Women
        in Love* completed. *Twilight
        in Italy* and *Amores*
        published. Medically
        examined (twice) for
        military service and
        declared unfit.

1917   Expelled from Cornwall as   Russian Revolution.
        suspected spies. Living in
        Berkshire and London.

Look! We Have Come Through!
published. *Aaron's Rod*
begun.

1918   Living in Derbyshire. Third
medical examination.
Publishes *New Poems* and
begins magazine publication
of *Studies in Classic American
Literature* and writes 'The
Fox'.

               End of First World War,
11 November.

1919   Leaves England for good
(except for three brief
visits). Living in Italy.
Publishes *Bay: A Book of
Poems*.

1920   Resumes work on *The Lost
Girl*. *Women in Love*
published in New York and
The Lost Girl (awarded the
James Tait Black Memorial
prize) in London. Living in
Sicily.

1921   In Sardinia, Germany,
Capri. Writes 'The
Captain's Doll' and 'The
Ladybird'. Publishes
*Movements in European
History, Psychoanalysis and the
Unconscious, Sea and Sardinia*

1922   In Ceylon, Australia,
California, New Mexico.
Settles at ranch in Lobo,
near Taos. *Kangaroo* begun.
*Aaron's Rod, Fantasia of the
Unconscious, England, my
England* published.

               T. S. Eliot's *The Waste Land*
published.

1923   Visits Mexico. Briefly in
London. Death of
Lawrence's father. *The
Plumed Serpent* begun. *The*

               Death of Katherine
Mansfield.

Ladybird, Studies in Classic American Literature, Kangaroo, Birds, Beasts and Flowers published.

1924	Returns to New Mexico. Seriously ill with tuberculosis. Visits Mexico again. *St Mawr* begun. *The Boy in the Bush* published.	E. M. Forster's *A Passage to India* published.
1925	Brief visit to London. Settles in Florence. *The Woman who Rode Away* and 'The Princess' begun. *St Mawr, Reflections on the Death of a Porcupine* published.	
1926	In London. Returns to Florence. *Lady Chatterley's Lover* begun. *The Plumed Serpent, David* published.	H. G. Wells' *The World of William Clissold* published. General Strike.
1927	Visits Etruria. *Mornings in Mexico* published.	
1928	Visits Switzerland (twice) and France. 'The Man Who Died' written. *The Woman Who Rode Away, Lady Chatterley's Lover, Collected Poems* published.	Death of Hardy. Bernard Shaw's *Intelligent Woman's Guide to Socialism and Capitalism* published.
1929	In France, Majorca, Germany and back in France. Paintings seized by police at exhibition, MS of *Pansies* by Customs. Wrote 'A Propos of Lady Chatterley's Lover', *Apocalypse* and 'The Ship of Death'. *The Paintings of D. H. Lawrence* and *Pansies* published.	

1930	Dies at Vence, Southern France 2 March.
1931	*Apocalypse* published.
1932	*Etruscan Places*, *The Letters* (ed. Huxley), *Last Poems*, published.
1933	*The Ship of Death* published.
1934	*The Tales* published.
1936	*Phoenix* published.

I Lawrence's life

Eastwood and Haggs Farm – 'The country of my heart'

The story of Lawrence's life has been told many times over but no one has written better about his childhood and early youth than Lawrence himself. In letters, essays, novels, stories, plays and poems, he returned over and over again to those much loved landscapes which lay in the curve of the river Erewash where it divides Nottinghamshire from Derbyshire. Long after he had left it for good, he evokes with poignant clarity the fields, streams and houses which made up what he called 'the country of my heart'. 'If you're ever in those parts again,' he writes to a correspondent towards the end of his life,

> go to Eastwood, where I was born, and lived for my first 21 years. Go to Walker St – and stand in front of the third house – and look across at Crich on the left, Underwood in front – High Park woods and Annesley on the right; I lived in that house from the age of 6 to 18, and I know that view better than any in the world. Then walk down the fields to the Breach, and in the corner house facing the stile I lived from 1 to 6.

Lawrence was nearly two when the family moved to the recently-built, colliery-owned end house on the Breach (called le Breche in ancient records). The new house had a strip of garden at the side and cost sixpence a week more in rent. The house in which Lawrence was born was in nearby Victoria Street, where the Lawrences had been living for nearly ten years before David Herbert Richards was born. Here Mrs Lawrence sold caps and aprons in the downstairs front room to help with the household expenses, always meagre and uncertain because her miner husband's pay varied from week to week and because he drank a good deal of it away. Before her marriage to Arthur John Lawrence, Lydia Beardsall had been a schoolteacher in Kent, was fond of reading, had written poetry and was deeply religious. Her father, a shipyard engineer in Sheerness since the failure of the Nottingham lace machine business where he had been working, was himself a devout Christian, a Wesleyan preacher with a passion for argument. Lydia Beardsall met Arthur Lawrence at a party given by one of her aunts who, as it happened, had married Arthur Lawrence's uncle. Thus Lawrence's parents already had mutual family connections when they met. Arthur's father lived in the mining village of Brinsley a mile from Eastwood; he was not himself a miner but company tailor to the colliery, making

the miners' pit-clothes. 'I remember,' Lawrence wrote in an auto-biographical essay in his last year, 'the great rolls of coarse flannel and pit-cloth which stood in the corner of my grandmother's shop when I was a small boy, and the big, strange old sewing-machine, like nothing else on earth, which sewed the massive pit-trousers. But when I was only a child the company discontinued supplying the men with pit-clothes.'

Lydia Beardsall had recently been jilted by her own 'young man' in favour of a wealthy widow. She was immediately drawn to the handsome, strong-bodied miner with flashing eyes and generous laugh and full black beard untouched by a razor. His speech, compounded of the dialects of Nottingham and Derbyshire, had for her the charm of an exotic language half understood, and his love of singing and dancing and enormous zest for life all conspired to captivate the genteel and soft-spoken ex-schoolmistress, as they had captivated so many others who knew him. Thirty years after Lawrence's father's death, an old miner still remembered him in Eastwood: ' . . . now there was a man. Full of life and friendliness. Big roaring carnation in his coat. They still talk about him in East-wood . . . He could dance, too, till his legs were broke to bits. He got buried.'

They were married at Sneinton parish church in December 1875, a few months after their first meeting, and moved to the house in Victoria Street, Eastwood very soon afterwards. During the next twelve years Lydia Lawrence bore two daughters and three sons. David Herbert, born on 11 September 1885 was the youngest of the sons and the youngest but one in the family.

Sons and Lovers portrays the Lawrences' marriage with unfading clarity and vigour and there are other first-hand accounts, such as that by Lawrence's sister Ada which go to show that in its broad outlines the fictional narrative corresponded to fact, at least as far as events were concerned. The marriage was not many months old before the pledge of total abstinence from drink given by the husband in the first flush of romantic ardour was broken and Arthur Lawrence rarely failed to stop at 'The Rising Sun' for a few pints on his way home. He was often careless at work and had to stay away due to injuries. This, together with the fact that his insolence to his imme-diate superiors resulted in him rarely getting a good 'stall' to work, further depleted the family's meagre income. In Lydia Lawrence's embittered mind the image of the handsome dancing stalwart she had met and fallen in love with faded rapidly, to be replaced by that of a selfish, drunken, penny-pinching boor, a bully and a liar to boot. And this was how she made the children see their father too.

The house in Victoria Street, Eastwood, where Lawrence was born on September 11, 1885.

The Lawrence family. Lawrence was the youngest of three sons and youngest but one in a family of five.

The quarrels between the parents became a dreaded yet familiar part of the children's lives. As they increased in intensity and frequency, the mother turned more and more to her sons for the warmth and understanding she no longer had from nor gave to her husband.

Lydia Lawrence determined that none of her sons would grow up to be like their father if she could help it, and all the evidence suggests that there was very little this frail but iron-willed woman could not help. The progressive changes of house, each time to a more genteel dwelling, were probably inspired by her. As the Breach ('the Bottoms' of *Sons and Lovers*) had been an improvement on Victoria Street ('Hell Row'), so the new house to which they moved when Lawrence was six was a step up on the social-topographical ladder. Lawrence nicknamed it Bleak House because it was exposed to the winds, being in Walker Street, at the top of the hilly ground that rose up from the Breach. Here Lawrence lived till he was eighteen and it is the view from here, towards Crich, Underwood and the Annesley Hills, which Lawrence said he knew better than any in the world. In 1902 the family moved to Lynn Croft Road, a semi-detached house rather than a terraced one like all the others.

But getting as far away as possible, physically and socially, from the ordinary miner's home was only a small, though important step in Lydia Lawrence's single-minded struggle to prevent her sons from following in their father's footsteps down the mine. The most powerful weapon the mother had to hand was education and she wielded it with ruthless and sustained efficiency. She personally supervised the progress at school of all her children, particularly the boys. The eldest, George (nine years older than D. H.), was first apprenticed to an uncle who was a picture-framer and later became a textile engineer, safely delivered from a future in the mines. But it was her second son, William Ernest, two years younger than George and seven years older than David, who was his mother's greatest delight as he was her supreme achievement. From the start William Ernest was as different from his father as even his mother could have wanted him to be. He inherited a good physique from his father, but there the resemblance ended. Well spoken, excellent at both sports and lessons, he left the Beauvale Board School loaded with prizes and certificates. His first job was at a colliery in Derbyshire, but as a clerk in the office, not a grimy coal-face worker like his father. From here Ernest went on to a better paid job at Langley Mill, west of Eastwood. His education continued under the close and constant encouragement of his mother. He went to night school to learn shorthand and typewriting and taught himself French and German with the help of correspondence courses. The reward of his unceasing efforts to better himself came when, after a brief stint at Coventry, he obtained a clerkship at a London shipping office. When he came down to Eastwood on holiday, elegantly attired in top hat, frock coat and gloves, he was the living symbol of his mother's vicarious triumph. As he walked down the high street with her on his arm, no one who did not know would have taken him for his miner father's son.

Young Bert, as he was called within the family, was constantly encouraged by his mother to follow his brother's example and strive for the same kind of success. As raw material for his mother's moulding the youngest son was every whit as promising as his brother, perhaps more so, for David had none of Ernest's athletic prowess. When he started at Beauvale School at the age of six or thereabouts, he was an unusually frail lad, 'a delicate, pale brat with a snuffy nose whom most people treated a mite gently' as he himself wrote many years later. (When he was born, his mother did not think he would survive.) But his treatment by his school mates seems to have been no gentler than that accorded to any sickly lad who disliked games and preferred the company of girls. 'Dicky Dicky Denches, Plays with the wenches' was the chant that accompanied him in chorus on at least one occasion, probably much oftener. Lawrence had two ways of retaliating against the rough treatment he received – to get back at them with his ferociously fluent and sarcastic tongue and to hurl himself into his studies with such fervour that he easily outperformed his fellows. Though he was always in the shadow of William Ernest during his years at Beauvale, he set a record for the school by being the first pupil to win a county scholarship to Nottingham High School, an ancient and prestigious institution. A schoolmate remembered him at this time as thin and pale with a high, girlish voice that rose in pitch when he became excited, which was often. Another recalled his chalk-white face and ginger hair and described Lawrence as the most effeminate and cowardly boy he ever knew. Already he had the little hacking cough which may have been the first sign of the disease which eventually killed him and the sharp movement of the left hand to the mouth which invariably accompanied it, a gesture which he never lost throughout his life.

Lawrence was twelve when he won the scholarship to Nottingham High School. His scholarship of twelve pounds barely covered his tuition and train fare, but his mother contrived to find whatever was needed to put her son through school by rigorous pruning of household expenses. Every school day for three years, Lawrence left home at seven in the morning to catch the train to school, returning at seven in the evening. The strain on his health must have affected his work for in his last year he was placed fifteenth out of nineteen boys, though earlier he had won both a form prize and a prize for mathematics. When he left school at seventeen (the normal school-leaving age and the end of formal education for boys who were not going up to University), Lawrence seemed set to follow in brother Ernest's footsteps, obtain a clerical post and, like him, be a credit to their mother. Indeed, it was Ernest who helped him draft the letter to a Nottingham surgical goods firm which resulted in David Herbert being employed as a clerk there at a salary of thirteen shillings a week.

And so, by dedicating herself unflinchingly to her self-appointed task, whatever the skimping, saving and sacrifices it required from herself and others, Mrs Lawrence had rescued the youngest son too from the terrible fate of going down the mine. But just when the mother's success seemed complete, tragedy struck with brutal swiftness. The brilliant and successful Ernest died in London of erysipelas complicated by pneumonia. By the time his mother reached his sick-bed (accompanied by the dazed father who was going up to London for the second time in his life) the bright and darling son was in a coma from which he never recovered. They brought him back to Eastwood, where he was buried on October 14, 1901. He was just twenty-three.

It was not surprising that some part of the mother too seemed to have died with the death of her beloved son. Lydia Lawrence withdrew into a blank stupor from which she was roused only by the fact that her youngest son too now fell ill with a severe attack of pneumonia. It seemed that he, who under the guidance of the mother had sedulously followed his brother, would now follow that brother to the grave. That danger shook the mother into life again. With all the ferocity of her frustrated passion she turned to the task of saving his life. Looking back many years later on this period, her eldest son remarked: 'my mother poured her very soul into him'.

She succeeded. When her iron devotion had saved his life (and perhaps her own), she clasped her younger son to her soul with a love which all but suffocated him, during the nine years of life still left to her. Lawrence had been at the surgical appliance factory only three months, though the experience he had there of narrowly avoiding being stripped naked by a group of factory girls seems to have disturbed him deeply. At any rate he did not return to the factory after his illness.

The summer before his brother died, he had formed a friendship with a family which was to provide the closest relationships of his early life, mother-love excepted. Ironically in the light of later events, it was through his mother that Lawrence first met Jessie Chambers, the 'Miriam' of *Sons and Lovers* and one of the three women who decisively affected his life. The Chambers family lived for three years in the Breach where Jessie's father had a milk round. The friendship between Mrs Lawrence and Mrs Chambers probably developed because both were in a sense outsiders, Mrs Chambers being a newcomer to the area and Lawrence's mother always considering herself different from the other miners' wives. When the Chambers moved to Haggs Farm, a few miles north-east of Eastwood, Mrs Chambers invited her friend to visit them in their new home. It was three years before the invitation was finally accepted and Mrs

Lawrence walked across the fields, along a short cut that no longer exists, to the Haggs – the Willey Farm of *Sons and Lovers*. Though the mother probably did not go to the farm again, the son became a regular visitor. But it was not, to begin with, the fourteen-year-old Jessie (two years younger than himself) who was the principal attraction for the young Lawrence. Rather it was the fresh and open world of the farm and the manifold activities involved in running it, activities into which the boy threw himself with characteristic energy. The farmer and his wife took to him at once and it was not long before the older boys, especially the eldest, Alan (George Saxton of *The White Peacock*), became his closest friends. All his life Lawrence loved to do simple physical things associated with country living – milking, baking bread and so on. It is at the Haggs that he had his first direct experience of this way of life. He had the capacity to enjoy everything he did at the farm – whether it was peeling potatoes, cleaning the fireplace or amusing the children. He had the even rarer gift of transmitting his own joy in physical activity to others. Something of his enormous zest for life – part of his paternal legacy – comes through in his own letters and in the reminiscences of those who knew him. 'Work goes like fun when Bert's there,' said the elder Chambers and Lawrence himself declared, in a letter to the youngest member of the Chambers family written two years before his death, 'Whatever else I am, I am somewhere still the same Bert who rushed with such joy to the Haggs.'

For Lawrence joining in the life of the farm, even merely visiting it, was an escape from the constant tension caused by parental strife and from the physical ugliness of Eastwood. At the beginning of the nineteenth century, Eastwood had less than one thousand inhabitants. A hundred years later there were nearly five thousand, most of them miners or small shopkeepers. There had been small scale coal mining in the area since the seventeenth century, but it was the Industrial Revolution which transformed the region, as it transformed so much of the Midlands and North. Though the nearest coal mine (where Lawrence senior worked) was at Brinsley, a mile away, mining and the mining company dominated the town. The shape, location and size of the houses, the life-style of most of the inhabitants, the clothes they wore most of the time, even the air they breathed – all had upon them the stamp of the colliery. For Lawrence it was a stamp of unrelieved ugliness: 'The real tragedy of England, as I see it, is the tragedy of ugliness. The country is so lovely: the man-made England is so vile. ... Now though perhaps nobody knew it, it was ugliness which betrayed the spirit of man, in the nineteenth century. The great crime which the moneyed classes and promoters of industry

Jessie Chambers, the Miriam of Sons and Lovers, *one of the three women who played a decisive part in Lawrence's life.*

committed in the palmy Victorian days was the condemning of the workers to ugliness, ugliness, ugliness: meanness and formless and ugly surroundings, ugly ideals, ugly religion, ugly hope, ugly love, ugly clothes, ugly furniture, ugly houses, ugly relationship between workers and employers. The human soul needs actual beauty even more than bread.' In the same late essay Lawrence says that to him the countryside around his home had always seemed extremely beautiful, 'still the old England of the forest and the agricultural past'. If, as he goes on to remark, the mines were to him 'an accident in the landscape', it was because it was so easy to get away from them, not only to the wooded countryside but especially to the warm and welcoming circle of the farming family of which he was almost a member himself.

The daughter of the family, Jessie Chambers, naturally enough found life on the farm less idyllic and soul-satisfying than the young escapee from the murk and grime of Eastwood. Though the parents were intelligent and cultured people (the father read out to the mother the instalments of *Tess of the D'Urbervilles* as they appeared each Saturday in the *Nottinghamshire Guardian*), her brothers seemed no more than affectionate boors who did not share her interest in books. In Lawrence she found a fellow enthusiast of equal or greater passion and seriousness towards things of the mind. Together they read and discussed a quite phenomenal number of books, most of them borrowed from the Mechanics' Institute at Eastwood. Fiction, poetry, autobiography, history, philosophy – under Lawrence's direction they eagerly devoured whatever they could find. The great English novelists – Dickens, George Eliot, Thackeray, Scott – opened up a vaster, more generous and exciting world than that which lay around them, as did the plays of Shakespeare and the poetry of Meredith, Browning and Swinburne. *The Golden Treasury* became a 'kind of Bible' and whatever they read together became not merely a text to be put away and forgotten but something to be felt in the blood and felt along the heart, something that entered immediately into the imaginative life which Lawrence and Jessie shared during the years of their close friendship, roughly the first decade of the new century. By the time Lawrence entered Nottingham University College to follow a teachers' training course his reading was far deeper and wider than that of most undergraduates (or graduates, for that matter) then or now.

In 1902, the Lawrences moved to the semi-detached house in Lynn Croft. Later that year Lawrence began work as a pupil teacher at the British School in Eastwood, on the invitation of the Reverend Reid, the Congregational minister who was a close friend of Mrs Lawrence. He did not enjoy his first experience of teaching any more than he did his later ones, but, encouraged by his mother, decided to carry on in his new calling. He attended a course for pupil teachers at nearby Ilkeston, where Jessie Chambers and a girl named Louise Burrows, to whom Lawrence was to be engaged a few years later, were also trainee teachers. These, together with one or two others, formed a social-intellectual group devoted to the discussion of radical ideas in art, politics and religion; they called themselves 'the Pagans'. For Jessie her two years at Ilkeston seemed in retrospect the happiest of her life.

A college education

Altogether Lawrence spent four years as a pupil teacher at Eastwood and Ilkeston, starting at £5 a year and earning £15 by the end. But the way forward as a teacher lay through examinations and certificates. At the end of 1904, he sat for the King's Scholarship examination, passed it with flying colours (he may have been first in the country) and qualified for a free place at a teacher training college. Six months later he passed the London Matriculation examination, which qualified him for admission to Nottingham University College. But he did not have the money for his fees, so he taught for a further year at Eastwood, putting aside most of his earnings to pay for his future expenses. Once more he was morally and practically supported by his mother. At the same time he coached Jessie for the King's Scholarship examination, which she sat in Easter 1906. In September of that year, at the age of twenty-one, Lawrence entered the University College to follow the teachers' training course. He had already begun work on the novel which was to become *The White Peacock*.

At one time he planned to take an external degree in Arts of London University (to which the University College of Nottingham was affiliated), but went back to his original course of studies when he found himself unable to obtain extra tuition in Latin. Lawrence enjoyed neither his teaching practice nor the formal education he was receiving at Nottingham. 'It had meant mere disillusion instead of the living contact of men,' he wrote later, and he dramatized the disillusion through Ursula's experience in *The Rainbow*. His relationship with Jessie Chambers was also deteriorating, not due to disillusionment on either side but to the fact that Lawrence was at this time almost completely dominated by his mother, emotionally though not intellectually. *Sons and Lovers* gives in part Lawrence's version of the end of his relationship with 'Miriam'. But Jessie Chambers' own memoir makes it clear that the spiritual, nun-like girl shying away from physical contact which the novel presents is at least in part a creation of Lawrence's imagination, shaped by his mother's fierce possessive love for her son. The relationship between Lawrence and Jessie was to drag on for four more years before it finally collapsed, but both knew long before that that it would never come to fruition. When Jessie came back from a holiday with the Lawrences in

My schoolmaster showed me the first issue of your paper, and I at once recognised its merits, and ordered one for myself. Needless to say, I have continued to take it ever since. I consider it of the greatest help to any student in our profession. I have always found that the courses of study contained in THE TEACHER have an originality which is very pleasing and instructive. The lessons on geography and history bring the important points clearly into view, and the mathematics

MR. D. H. LAWRENCE

are splendid practice to anyone who would have every rule in its different forms at his command. Especially valuable are the Science and English, the former being particularly adapted for those who cannot enjoy the benefits of a laboratory. I consider the TEACHER a first class magazine for teachers ; it is eminently practical and yet has an intellectual chatty tone which is very charming.

During my study I used:—*English:* Evan Daniel, and Meiklejohn ; *History:* Ransome and Gardiner ; *Arithmetic:* Christian and Collar ; *Geography:* Gill and Meiklejohn. I have been teaching for two years and a half, and until March of last year received my instruction from Mr. G. Holderness, headmaster of the Eastwood British School. In that month. however, I obtained permission to attend the Ilkeston Centre, and there I received the greatest assistance from the Principal, Mr. T. A. Beacroft.

The earliest photograph of Lawrence to appear in print. From The Teacher, *March 25, 1905.*

Mablethorpe in the summer of 1906, her life had been completely changed by the realization that Lawrence could never really love her. In the meantime his friendship with Louise Burrows, also a student at the college, was growing rapidly, though not perhaps deepening. He debated with himself whether he could marry Louise 'from the purely animal side'. On Jessie's twenty-first birthday, January 1908, he wrote to her saying he could love 'the deep spirit within' her (Jessie) all his life but that he could only give her what he 'would give a holy nun. So you must let me marry a woman I can kiss and embrace and make the mother of my children.'

Lawrence's first appearance in print as a creative writer occurred during his second year at the college (the college magazine had rejected a poem he had sent in); it was not under his own name but that of Jessie Chambers. The *Nottinghamshire Guardian* ran a Christmas competition in 1907, offering a prize of three pounds for the best Christmas story under each of three sections. Partly to earn something towards his college expenses, Lawrence decided to submit stories for all three sections; but since entries were limited to one per competitor, he persuaded Jessie Chambers and Louise Burrows to put their names to two of the stories. 'A Prelude', submitted under Jessie's name, won one of the prizes. Jessie Chambers was also responsible for sending some of Lawrence's poems to *The English Review*, where they were published and led to Lawrence's introduction to the London literary world. But this was not till two and a half years later. Before that Lawrence had completed his training course, being told that he had obtained a distinction in all subjects except English. He read particularly widely in philosophy during the latter part of his stay at college, not always as part of his course of studies. Among the philosophers who especially interested him were Locke, John Stuart Mill, Darwin, William James and the Schopenhauer of *The World as Will and Idea*. Two years after leaving Nottingham, he wrote to one of the lecturers there: 'you showed me the way out of a torturing, crude monism, past pragmatism, into a sort of crude but appealing pluralism'. He had ceased to be a believing Christian several years earlier, even before he was a member of 'the Pagans'.

Croydon and London: from teaching to writing

If he had to be a schoolteacher, Lawrence was determined that he would at least name his own price. He would not take any teaching job that paid less than £90 a year. After one or two disappointments, he found a job in the newly opened Davidson Road School at Croydon.

Lawrence was a conscientious teacher and his educational ideas were both imaginative and sound, and well in advance of educational orthodoxy at the time. For instance, he encouraged drama in the classroom, and he even persuaded some of the boys he taught to produce compositions which he revised and submitted to boys' magazines, sharing out the small sums received among the young contributors. But he did not enjoy his years at Croydon, though he worked under a headmaster who let him teach in his own way without direction or interference, and had at least one colleague, A. W. McLeod, who shared his passion for literature and ideas. At the beginning he suffered from intense homesickness and several of his earliest published poems deal with this theme. When this had worn off he still found he could not believe enough in what he was doing to commit himself wholeheartedly to it. There were about sixty boys in his class, the usual number at the time. He said he could instruct a hundred, but doubted whether he could educate a dozen. Without his mother's encouragement, he would probably not have become a schoolteacher (as she herself had been). Now that he had become one, he felt frustrated and ill at ease, both because he found the daily drudgery and particularly the maintenance of discipline in the classroom irksome, and also because his emotional affairs were in a state of uncertainty. He still corresponded with Jessie and Louise, and was soon to ask Jessie to meet a third girl whom he was considering marrying, though physical sex seems to have been a more urgent objective at this time than marriage. But throughout the petty frustrations of his job and his emotional restlessness, the ambition of being a writer remained constant. He worked steadily at *The White Peacock* (at first called *Laetitia* and later *Nethermere*), and also wrote several poems. He sent the various instalments of his novel as well as some poems to Jessie for comment, although he told another female correspondent, Blanche Jennings, that Jessie was 'valueless as a critic' because 'she approves too much'.

Jessie approved enough, at any rate, to submit some of Lawrence's poems (choosing for him the pseudonym Richard Greasley) to *The English Review* in June 1909. The first number of the journal under the editorship of Ford Madox Hueffer (later Ford Madox Ford) had appeared the previous December and Lawrence, who was home for the Christmas holidays, had taken a copy down to Haggs Farm. Lawrence was on holiday in the Isle of Wight when Jessie received a letter from Ford inviting Lawrence to visit him in London. He did so in September and wrote to Jessie almost immediately after the meeting, describing Ford as 'fairish, fat, about forty, and the kindest man on earth'. Ford's version of his first encounter with Lawrence and his work is more colourful but less reliable. He describes how Lawrence came into his office 'looking like a red fox' and how, by the time he met him, he had already decided that Lawrence was a genius. According to Ford, Jessie had sent him not only poems by Lawrence, but a short story, 'The Odour of Chrysanthemums'. As soon as he read it, he put it in the 'accepted manuscripts' file and left for a dinner party where the assembled guests included Maurice Baring, Hillaire Belloc, G. K. Chesterton and H. G. Wells. At one point, according to Ford, Wells remarked 'Hooray! Fordie's discovered another genius! Called D. H. Lawrence!'

The story is true in spirit and deserves to be so in the letter, for it was through Ford that Lawrence gained admission to the literary world of metropolitan London. Though Ford later confessed that he had never really liked Lawrence much because even when he got to know him well he remained too disturbing, he was unstintingly generous with his literary patronage. During the year in which he was editor, *The English Review* published work by most of the established authors of the day – Wells, Bennett, Conrad, James, Hardy – as well as the work of younger writers such as Ezra Pound, Wyndham Lewis and Edward Thomas. Many of these writers and others Lawrence first met through Ford. It is clear from various contemporary accounts that the tall, thin, somewhat shabbily clad provincial with the vivid blue eyes, the shock of dark hair and the small ginger moustache (the famous fox-red beard was to come later) made a strong impression on most of those who met him. At the very beginning it was of course the man rather than the writer who made his impact on literary and artistic London as *The White Peacock* had not yet been published. It is perhaps a mark of Ford's confidence in his new discovery that the issue of the magazine in which Lawrence's poems were printed gave him pride of place in a list of contributors which included such eminent Edwardians as John Galsworthy, R. B. Cunninghame Graham and Henry Nevinson.

As a writer, Lawrence seems to have known almost from the very beginning the path he wished to follow. With his first novel and some of the subsequent ones he showed a great readiness to chop and change, and was seeking advice not only from literary men such as Ford (and later Edward Garnett), but from friends and acquaintances like Jessie Chambers and Blanche Jennings. But while he was willing and even eager to shape his early work to suit the fashions and taboos of the Edwardian literary and publishing world, he was always clearsighted as to just what he was doing, and, on some matters, quite adamant.

It took Lawrence three years to get *The White Peacock* into its final form, and the novel was not published until early in 1911. But before that he was able to obtain a copy especially bound up to put into the hands of his beloved mother who was dying of cancer. She looked at the outside, then at the title page, then at her son who was at her bedside, and the book was put down. Lawrence's sister read out the inscription he had written for her. She never spoke of the book or looked at it again.

Ford Madox Ford – 'fairish, fat, about forty, and the kindest man on earth'.

Lydia Lawrence during her final illness.

His father's comment was far more forthright. On being told that Lawrence had received £50 for the novel, he exclaimed: 'And tha's niver done a day's work in thy life!'

Mrs Lawrence died in December 1910 after five months of slowly increasing agony. Lawrence described the year that followed as his 'sick year'. He had become engaged to Louise Burrows about the time of his mother's death (Mrs Lawrence's animosity towards Jessie was constant and undiminished), but clearly the emotional centre of his life had gone. He did very little writing during that year, though before his first novel was published he had written early versions of both *The Trespasser* and *Sons and Lovers*. The former was based on the experience of another Croydon teacher, Helen Corke (not a colleague), who had had a love affair with a married musician who afterwards committed suicide. She wrote her own fictional version of the relationship in *Neutral Ground*, published twenty-one years after *The Trespasser*. During his first year at Croydon, and immediately after the shock which Helen Corke suffered in the autumn of 1909 when her lover killed himself, her relationship with Lawrence reached its peak. He was a sympathetic and understanding friend, but though he wanted physical sex with her (he even proposed to her), she refused. In addition to *The Trespasser*, Helen Corke figures in several short stories as well as in Lawrence's early 'Helen' poems. In 1968, when she was eighty-six, Helen Corke spoke of the great affection and sympathy she had felt for Lawrence and remarked on how attractive she had found Jessie Chambers. The two women became fast friends, though Helen Corke's friendship with Lawrence did not outlast the three years during which they knew each other at Croydon.

Looking back much later on that dark year following his mother's death, Lawrence wrote how 'for me everything collapsed, save the mystery of death, and the haunting of death in life. I was twenty-five, and from the death of my mother, the world began to dissolve around me, beautiful, iridescent, but passing away substanceless. Till I almost dissolved away myself, and was very ill'. When he went home to Eastwood for the Easter holidays, he did not want to see anyone except his family and close friends.

The White Peacock was by no means badly received, but Lawrence could not hope as yet to earn his living as a writer. He continued to put most of his spare time and energy into his writing, but his health was poor and he was becoming increasingly frustrated with teaching at Croydon. He was also doing a certain amount of painting at this time, mainly copying other artists' work in watercolours. For some time he considered trying to find employment in the Midlands where his fiancee was teaching, but does not appear to have explored this idea very deeply. In the meantime, the publication of *The White Peacock* opened more doors for him in London's literary and social world. Earnest Rhys, the founder of Everyman's Library, has

Helen Corke. Lawrence met her while teaching in Croydon and based The
Trespasser *on a relationship between her and a married musician who later
committed suicide.*

recorded one occasion at a party in his Hampstead home where Yeats, Pound, the actress Florence Farr and others recited poems. Lawrence, when invited to read some of his, read for over half an hour from a little notebook, with his back to the company 'in an expressive, not very audible voice' till there were restless murmurs and the host politely asked the young poet to have a little rest.

In the autumn of 1911, while he was staying at his fiancée's home in Leicestershire, Lawrence had a letter from Edward Garnett, a member of a famous literary family and editor for the publishing house of Gerald Duckworth. Next to Hueffer (who seems to have lost interest in Lawrence after he had discovered and launched him), Garnett was Lawrence's most influential literary acquaintance, and, during the difficult time when Lawrence and Frieda first ran away together, a sympathetic and generous friend. Garnett's letter was written on behalf of *The Century*, an American magazine, and inquired whether Lawrence had any short stories ready. Lawrence was now working on the book that was to become *Sons and Lovers*. Earlier that year he had already submitted the manuscript of *The Trespasser* (originally titled *The Saga of Siegmund*) to Heinemann, who had published his first novel. But he had serious reservations about the new work and asked for the return of the manuscript, telling Heinemann's reader that he had resolved not to publish it in its then state and not at all for some years, though it eventually appeared the following year.

Lawrence not only sent Jessie the early draft of *Sons and Lovers* (then called *Paul Morel*), with which she was not overly impressed, but asked her to write out her recollections of their early relationship, which he used in revising and rewriting the novel. When Garnett's letter arrived, he had already promised a volume of short stories to another publisher who had asked for them for the following spring, though he had by then written a mere half dozen, including the three submitted for the *Nottinghamshire Guardian* Christmas competition. But he was able to send Garnett two stories within a fortnight. He was invited to the Garnetts' country farmhouse, the Cearne, in Kent and made several visits there that autumn, often going down for the weekend. On one of his visits he was caught in a shower which turned his cold into a serious attack of pneumonia. 'I must leave school, really,' he wrote to Garnett in early November, on the very day on which he taught at Croydon for the last time.

Lawrence continued working on the manuscript of *The Trespasser* during the rest of that year and into the next, while convalescing. He had promised that he would not publish the book without Helen Corke's consent, which he now obtained. Duckworth's published it in May 1912 and it had a cooler reception than his first novel, though few of the critics were as severe as Lawrence himself had been, especially of his earlier drafts. Even before he finished it, he thought the novel 'too florid, too chargé'; though he added, 'it can't be anything else – it is itself. I must let it stand'. He was still busily working on the *Sons and Lovers* manuscript as well as on some short stories. *The English Review*, now under the editorship of Austin Harrison, continued to publish his poems and stories. By 1912, therefore, the choice between teaching and writing had been made for Lawrence by force of circumstances. Teaching had proved physically too demanding. And his relationship with Louie Burrows was slowly reaching withering- rather than breaking-point. His letters to her do not suggest that he ever treated her as an intellectual or emotional equal. (Helen Corke had been surprised that he had become engaged to someone for whose mind he evidently had no respect.) In February 1912 Lawrence asked Louie to release him from the engagement.

Frieda Weekley: 'The woman of a lifetime'

If 1911 had been Lawrence's 'sick year', the succeeding one was to be a year of radiant and abundant life for both the man and the writer. Officially, he was still on the staff of Davidson Road school (till mid-March), but he now devoted his time to rewriting *Sons and Lovers* on which he accepted several suggestions from Jessie. She met him often during this period and felt his mother's grip on him to be stronger than ever.

One of Lawrence's aunts, who had married a German scholar, had invited him to join them on a holiday in Germany so that he could explore the possibility of finding a job as Lektor in a German university. It was to get help in this project that he visited his former instructor in French at Nottingham University College, Professor Ernest Weekley. The visit took place in early April, 1912. At Weekley's home in Mapperly, Nottingham, Lawrence met his wife, Frieda, a member of an aristocratic German family and a distant cousin of the First World War air ace Manfred von Richthofen. She was thirty-two when she first saw Lawrence, 'a long thin figure, quick straight legs, light sure movements. He seemed so obviously simple.' She herself was a well-built, attractive blonde with greenish brown eyes, a love of company and a capacity for enjoyment which her married life left largely unfulfilled. Disappointed in her existence as a provincial bourgeois housewife, she had sunk, after twelve years of marriage, into a kind of 'sleepwalking through the days', to use her own phrase. By the standards of her day, she was an emancipated woman with very liberal ideas and a forthright way of expressing them, and had little in common with the rather severe English

Frieda Weekley in 1912, the year Lawrence first met her.

philologist from a dissenting background whom she had met and married while on holiday in the Black Forest. She had a son and two daughters when Lawrence, then twenty-seven, first met her.

The relationship between the young provincial painfully making his way into a higher social sphere and the disappointed aristocrat turned bourgeois developed rapidly, though it would be quite misleading to account for it entirely in terms of the attraction of social opposites. Over and over again those who met Lawrence have commented on the vivid awareness that quickened his whole personality and made his poor health seem a grotesque irrelevance almost until his death. There is little doubt that it was to this quality in him above all that Frieda responded. At first she found it difficult to take the directness of Lawrence's attitude, as when he rebuked her for her ignorance in being unable to make tea because she did not know how to light the gas. Frieda soon realized that she loved him. 'He had touched a new tenderness in me.' She invited him to spend the night with her at her home on Sunday when her husband was away, an invitation which Lawrence firmly refused. He insisted that they should tell the husband and go away together. Frieda was torn between her love for the children and the promise of a new and fuller life with Lawrence, a conflict which raged within her long after they had gone away together and which at one time threatened to destroy their union. The thought of the social scandal she might cause, if it occurred to her at all, seems only to have spurred her on. As for Lawrence, his reaction to her was immediate and unambiguous. 'She is ripping – she is the finest woman I've ever met,' he wrote to Garnett exultantly; 'Oh, but she's the woman of a lifetime'. On 3 May 1912, Lawrence and Frieda left England for Germany.

Frieda had undertaken to tell her husband of her plans but had not done so. She left her son at home and took the two girls to their grandparents at Hampstead. She and Lawrence crossed the Channel on their way to her home town of Metz, to which she had already planned a visit to join in the celebrations for the fiftieth anniversary of her father's entry into military and public service. The house was full of relatives, which made it easier for her to stay at a hotel, in spite of her mother's wish that she should stay in the family home. She and Lawrence took separate rooms. Lawrence had just eleven pounds to pay for all their expenses. While Frieda was explaining the situation to her family, Lawrence was arrested as a suspected British spy and Baron von Richthofen had to intervene to obtain his release. When Frieda took Lawrence home to meet her parents shortly after, the atmosphere was one of hostile politeness on the father's part.

Lawrence tried to work on *Paul Morel* while he waited but, understandably, did not make much progress with it. He wrote a letter to Weekley and insisted once more that Frieda told him everything, either by sending his letter or on her own. 'I love you. Let us face anything, put up with anything. But this crawling under the mud I cannot bear.'

On his release from custody, Lawrence travelled northward along the Mosel to Trier and thence to his German uncle's sister's home at Waldbröl, near Bonn, where he continued work on his novel and flirted mildly with his married cousin. He met Frieda again in Munich, at the house of her sister Else who was married to a professor of political economy at the university. They had an eight-day 'honeymoon' in the beautiful countryside along the Isar, against the backdrop of the blue Tyrolean alps. Else's lover, another university professor, had lent them a small flat in the village of Icking and here they lived on black bread, eggs and fruit while Lawrence revised his novel and wrote several poems dealing with their relationship. To both of them it seemed almost literally as if they had been reborn into a new life. In her autobiography *Not I But the Wind*, Frieda wrote of those early ecstatic days: 'I didn't want people, I didn't want anything, I only wanted to revel in this new world Lawrence had given me', while Lawrence himself wrote to a friend at Nottingham: 'The world is wonderful and beautiful and good beyond one's wildest imagination. Never, never, never could one conceive what love is, beforehand, never. Life can be great – quite god-like. It *can* be so. God be thanked I have proved it.'

Journey into Italy

But their happiness was not entirely unclouded. Frieda's husband refused to give her a divorce and the news that her children were unhappy made Frieda tense with grief and anxiety. She had gone back to look after her sister Else's children in a nearby village and Lawrence fretted at their separation and her longing. There were many bitter quarrels.

Edward Garnett's son, who was on holiday in Germany, came to see Lawrence at his father's suggestion and together they walked to Wolfratshausen to see Frieda. Shortly afterwards Lawrence and Frieda began a trek southwards to Italy, but not before the Frau Baronin, Frieda's mother, had arrived and berated Lawrence roundly for expecting a baron's daughter to wait on him and live like a barmaid while he could not even afford to keep her in shoes. But she spoke in praise of Lawrence to her elder daughter when she arrived in Munich very soon afterwards.

Lawrence had by now abandoned his plan of getting a teaching post in Germany and decided to be a full-time writer. The lovers set off together on foot in mid-August with rucksacks on their backs, having sent their luggage on ahead to Lago di Garda. They carried a spirit lamp for cooking and slept in hay huts in the mountains, experiences memorably rendered by Lawrence in *Love Among the Haystacks*. They had £23 between them and it took them three weeks to reach Riva at the northern tip of Lake Garda, climbing over the Pfitzerjoch pass and down through Merano, Bolzano and Trento, all then in Austrian territory. David Garnett and later Harold Hobson joined them for part of the walking tour and Garnett has recounted Lawrence's great good spirits and his wonderful displays of mimicry, both of himself and others, including Yeats and Pound, as well as the keen botanical interests he shared with Garnett. 'Though I saw a great deal of Lawrence in the three or four years that followed, whenever he was in England,' Garnett has written, 'I never saw him so well or so happy, so consistently gay and light-hearted.' During this tour Lawrence wrote some of the poems which later appeared in *Look! We Have Come Through!*, an autobiographical collection dealing with the early days of his relationship with Frieda, as well as some essays, the best known and best of which is 'Christs in the Tirol'.

Before he had left Germany, Lawrence had submitted the manuscript of *Paul Morel* to Heinemann, who rejected it, because he thought it was a dirty book, according to Lawrence. He then sent it to Edward Garnett at Duckworth's. Garnett sent the manuscript back with detailed suggestions for revision and Lawrence set about rewriting the novel, working on it throughout their walking tour and completing it in November 1912. A few days after their arrival in Riva (where they cooked their meals secretly in a cheap hotel room to save money, hiding the spirit lamp under the bed when the maid came in), Lawrence had a cheque for £50 from Duckworths and Frieda received new clothes from her sister. They travelled further south to Gargnano, an isolated village set in olive groves and vineyards which at that time could only be reached by water. Here they rented a flat on the first floor of a villa and, in Frieda's words 'Lawrence for the first time had a place of his own'. It cost three guineas a month and they lived there till the following April. Frieda set about learning to be an efficient housekeeper and a good cook (Lawrence had been responsible for what cooking they did up to this time), while Lawrence spent most of his time writing and occasionally painting.

By the new year he had written a new play, *Fight for Barbara*, based on the Frieda–Lawrence–Weekley situation, and had begun work on *The Lost Girl* which was not published till 1920. In February a collection of his early poems came out under the title *Love Poems and Others* and Lawrence sent a copy to Jessie Chambers. He also sent her the proofs of *Sons and Lovers* (the title he now settled on, in consultation with Garnett, for the 'Paul Morel' novel) and invited

Map showing some of the places visited by Lawrence and Frieda during their walking tour in 1912; they settled in Gargnano for several months.

Journey into Italy, 1912

GERMANY

● München

● Wolfratshausen

● Salzburg

AUSTRIA

● Innsbruck

Drenner Pass ● Pfitzerjoch

● Vipiteno

● Merano

DOLOMITES

● Bolzano

TYROL

● Trento

● Riva

● Gargnano

Lago di Garda

● Brescia

● Milan

● Verona

● Venice

ITALY

N

0   50 miles

0   80 km

her comments. She declined when she realized that in spite of her earlier suggestions the portrayal of herself as Miriam was essentially unchanged. At this time Lawrence also began work on a novel which was to have had as its central figure a character like Robert Burns but in a Derbyshire setting. He abandoned this after writing a few pages and began work on the most important literary production to come out of his stay in Gargnano. This was a novel, originally called *The Sisters*, which he began as a 'pot boiler', but which, after long and extensive revision and rewriting, grew into Lawrence's two masterpieces *The Rainbow* and *Women in Love*.

Return to England

Early in April they moved to a farm-house in nearby San Gaudenzio where they shared lodgings with the woman who first gave Lawrence the name by which many female admirers were to call him, Lorenzo. 'It is quite wonderful and unspoilt everywhere,' he writes to David Garnett. 'There are little grape hyacinths standing about, and peach blossom is pink among the grey olives, and cherry blossom shakes in the wind. Oh, my sirs, what more do you want.'

From here they made their way to Germany, on their way to England. They had decided to return in order to do whatever they could to get the matter of the divorce settled as soon as possible. In Germany they stayed at a holiday home in Irschenhausen, outside Munich. It belonged to Frieda's sister Else, and her husband, Professor Jaffe. All the time he was away from England Lawrence had tried to keep in touch with contemporary English fiction through reading books sent him by his former Croydon colleague A. W. McLeod. He had read Arnold Bennett's *Anna of the Five Towns* and been repelled by what he considered Bennett's essentially negative outlook. 'I hate Bennett's resignation,' he had written to McLeod. Conrad's *Under Western Eyes* bored him and reading H. G. Wells' *The New Machiavelli* in Irschenhausen depressed him intensely: 'And I do so break my heart over England when I read *The New Machiavelli*. And I am sure that only through a readjustment between men and women, and a making free and healthy of the sex, will she get out of her present atrophy.' Partly through personal experience both painful and joyously liberating, partly through the new perspective on England and English life given him by his Continental sojourn and partly as a reaction against what he saw as the stifling irrelevance of novelists such as Bennett and Wells (though earlier he had greatly admired *Tono Bungay*), Lawrence was slowly beginning to recognize and mark out the area of experience he was to make uniquely his own in modern English fiction. Before he left Irschenhausen he wrote at length to Edward Garnett, apropos of the fact that *Love Poems and Others* had sold only one hundred copies and that Duckworth might be hesitating over *Sons and Lovers*: 'I *know* I can write bigger stuff than any man in England. And I have to write what I can write.' Later in the same letter he insisted: 'I can only write what I feel pretty strongly about; and that, at present, is the relations between men and women. After all, it is *the* problem of today.'

In Germany he was perhaps becoming aware of other problems, such as the first rumblings of the war that was to burst upon Europe the following year. At any rate he did not like his stay in Germany this time as he had done on his first visit. During his stay he wrote some of the stories which were later to be collected as *The Prussian Officer*, a title devised by Garnett which Lawrence disliked – 'Garnett was a devil to call my book *The Prussian Officer*,' he wrote to his agent when the book was published in 1914, 'what Prussian Officer?'

Lawrence and Frieda were back in England in June. They stayed with the Garnetts at the Cearne and later at Kingsgate on the Kentish coast. Garnett had sent Lawrence the reviews of *Sons and Lovers*, which were generally very favourable. The book was not a financial success but Lawrence was now very much an important young author. Through the Garnetts they met the critic John Middleton Murry and the New Zealand-born short story writer Katherine Mansfield. Like Lawrence and Frieda, Murry and Katherine were living together though they were not married. Lawrence and the Murrys were to have an intense, stormy and finally frustrating relationship, amply documented on both sides as well as by innumerable interested onlookers. At this time Lawrence also made the acquaintance of Edward Marsh, editor of *Georgian Poetry*, who was to publish some of his poems and with whom Lawrence later had a running battle about poetry, especially poetic metre. Marsh introduced Lawrence to Herbert Asquith, the son of the Prime Minister, and to his wife, Cynthia, an introduction which was to prove invaluable during the time, after the outbreak of war, when Lawrence and Frieda underwent severe harassment, even persecution. Cynthia Asquith came to have a place of special importance in Lawrence's life and imagination, though contrary to family suspicions at the time, they did not have an affair.

At Kent, Lawrence and Frieda were frequent visitors at the Broadstairs home of the younger Asquiths. Nothing could be done about the divorce, and Frieda was deeply disappointed that she could not be with her children more, and Lawrence was less than sympathetic. The tension between them flared out into open quarrelling. Lawrence was quite ill at this time, occasionally coughing blood. He paid a brief visit to Eastwood for his sister Ada's visit. He did not do much writing that summer, and Edward Marsh said of him at the time, 'He looks terribly ill, which I am afraid he is.' To a visitor to Kingsgate he said, striking his chest violently, 'I've something here, savage, that is heavier than concrete. If I don't get it out it will kill me.' But in spite of, or perhaps because of, his physical illness, almost everyone who met him was instantly and vividly aware of the powerful life-energy which animated the sickly frame, at times so intensely that it threatened to destroy it. 'I doubt if anyone could have been in Lawrence's presence for two minutes,' wrote Cynthia Asquith, 'without being struck by his difference from other people. It was not a difference of degree; it was a difference of kind. Some electric, elemental quality gave him a flickering radiance. Apart from his strange otherness, one could see at once that he was preternaturally alive.'

By August, Lawrence and Frieda were back at Irschenhausen, staying with the Jaffes. Here Lawrence was able to get back to his writing and worked with feverish energy on the proofs of his Italian essays and a play *The Widowing of Mrs Holroyd*, the manuscript of which Garnett had kept for a long time. He was also making slow progress with *The Sisters*. This time Germany seemed refreshing after England. 'I can't tell you how glad I am to be out of England again,' he wrote to Garnett. 'Everything seems so living: so quick. . . . I feel as if not once, all the time I was in England, had I really wakened up.' But his gaze was fixed on Italy, on 'the Mediterranean, and the mountains, and my beloved Italy,' as he put it in a letter written from Irschenhausen to an Eastwood friend.

Italy, and England again: marriage

While Frieda went to visit her parents in Metz, Lawrence began a two-week walking tour through Switzerland and into Italy. He did not care for Switzerland – 'am cured of that little country for ever. The only excitement in it is that you can throw a stone a frightfully long way down – that is forbidden by law.' He also found the mountains at close quarters merely obtrusive, and the signs of industrialization depressed him. Milan was 'beastly' and he was put off both by the 'imitation hedgehog of a cathedral' and the 'hateful town Italians', though he later came to recognize a vividness and vigour beneath what he saw as the outward 'mechanization' of the latter's lives.

Frieda joined him in Milan and they rented a small house in the little fishing village of Lerici, where they lived for eight months. Once more it was an idyllic setting, a little pink house set in a garden with vines and figs and wild crocus, looking out from the olive-covered mountain side to the pale blue sea dotted with little fishing boats. But Frieda was still upset about her children and again Lawrence's writing went very slowly. The very enchantment of the setting seemed to inhibit creative work, as he told Garnett. 'But here it is too beautiful, one can't work.'

The literary success of *The White Peacock* and *Sons and Lovers* had made Lawrence fairly well known and there were frequent visits from British people living in the area as well as from visiting artists and literary people, among them Edward Marsh and Constance Garnett, Edward's wife and translator of Dostoievsky.

In spite of distractions and interruptions, Lawrence managed to finish one draft of *The Sisters* by May 1914. But at Lerici most of his energy seems to have gone into trying to establish a firm and good relationship with Frieda and into literary-critical arguments with Marsh and Garnett. There were the usual worries about money and these were not eased when a cheque for £35 from an American publisher for *Sons and Lovers* could not be cashed locally because of an altered date.

In the early months of the new year Lawrence was beginning to get more deeply and continuously involved in his new novel (now called *The Wedding Ring*) which he sent to Garnett in two instalments. Garnett did not like the book and there was a spirited exchange between them over its nature and merits. In the meantime Weekley had finally agreed to a divorce and on 28 May 1914, a decree *nisi* was granted. Frieda and Lawrence immediately made plans to return. She went back to Metz to see her dying father for the last time while Lawrence once more walked through Switzerland via the St Bernard's Pass and Interlaken, then westward into France and so to England. He was accompanied by an engineer named Lewis who worked at Spezia in the Vickers-Maxim factory. By late June Lawrence and Frieda were reunited in England. They stayed in London with Gordon Campbell, a young barrister with literary interests whom they had met through the Murrys on their earlier visit. On 13 July 1914, Frieda and Lawrence were married at the Kensington Register Office. The witnesses were Murry and Campbell. 'I don't feel a changed man, but I suppose I am one,' Lawrence wrote immediately afterwards.

During his stay in London, Lawrence came to know Dr David Eder, one of the pioneers of Freudian theory in England, and his sister-in-law Barbara Low who also became a well-known psycho-analyst. Eder had been interested in Lawrence after reading *Sons and Lovers* and called on him frequently and, according to Barbara Low, Lawrence was greatly impressed by Eder's exposition of Freudian ideas, though chary of being influenced by anything that smacked of a 'science'. This was Lawrence's first formal contact, so to speak, with Freudian psychological notions, though Frieda had been familiar with some of them for several years. In 1907 she had had an affair lasting several years with Otto Gross, a disciple of Freud. During this time Lawrence also met the novelist Richard Aldington and his wife Hilda Doolittle ('H. D.') and the American Imagist poet Amy Lowell, an encounter which left Lawrence feeling

The Lawrences' wedding, July 13, 1914. Katherine Mansfield (2nd from left) and John Middleton Murry (end right) were the witnesses.

that it was 'an almost hopeless business' to try to publish poetry in the literary climate of London at the time.

The nightmare of the war years

Through Edward Marsh, who was secretary to Winston Churchill at the Admiralty, Lawrence had heard of the possible outbreak of war with Germany. On the last day of July he set off on a walking tour with Lewis, the Vickers engineer who had accompanied him through Switzerland and France, and four others including S. S. Koteliansky, a Russian emigré who became a close friend of Lawrence if not of Frieda. They planned to go to the Lake District. After that Lawrence intended to go to Ireland with the Campbells or back to Germany because, as he told Mrs H. G. Wells on the day the walking tour began, he was tired of London.

Lewis' home was in Barrow in Furness and there, on August 5, the party heard the news that war had been declared. At first, he recalled, 'we all went mad'. In the same letter, written five months after the event, to Cynthia Asquith he writes: 'It seems like another life. We *were* happy – four men. . . . And since then, since I came back, things have not existed for me. . . . And nobody existed, because I did not exist myself.'

The outbreak of war made it impossible for the moment to go back to the Continent and the projected trip to Ireland did not materialize. Lawrence had to look around for somewhere to live and for money. Duckworth had been reluctant to publish the new novel but an agent had secured for Lawrence the offer of £300 for it, though the money was a long time coming. The Lawrences rented a cottage in Chesham, Buckinghamshire for six shillings a month and Lawrence began work on a study of Thomas Hardy which he had planned some time before war broke out. The cottage was damp and he was often ill and they left after five months. This was the time he looked back on in the letter quoted above. While at Chesham they met Gilbert Cannan, a popular novelist of the day who lived nearby and through him Compton Mackenzie and Mark Gertler, a young painter who became a close friend. The Murrys also had a cottage at Lee, three miles away.

In December *The Prussian Officer* was published and the Lawrences paid a visit to his sister Ada in Derbyshire. By this time Lawrence was very well known in literary circles and in the upper reaches of the London social world, through people like Marsh and the Asquiths. Viola Meynell, the daughter of the Catholic poet Alice Meynell, offered the Lawrences her cottage at Greatham near Pulborough in Sussex and in January they moved into it. Lawrence was still busy revising his novel (which he had now decided to call *The Rainbow*) and had also become interested, in reaction to what he saw as the massive and monstrous inhumanity of the war, in the idea of a small community of chosen people living a simple but intense life of cooperation and communion. It was an idea which was to haunt him throughout his life, though his commitment to it varied sharply at different times.

They lived in Greatham for six months and it was here that Lawrence came into direct contact with the so-called Bloomsbury circle, that group of writers, artists and thinkers based mainly in London and Cambridge who dictated the tone of intellectual life in London in the years immediately following the war. Bertrand Russell, who was a fervent pacifist at the time (his views were to cost him his fellowship at Trinity College, Cambridge the following year), came to see Lawrence at Cambridge, accompanied by Lady Ottoline Morrell, whose lover Russell then was. Lady Ottoline was an eccentric and colourful personality who saw herself as patroness of literature and the arts in the grand Augustan manner. Her house, Garsington Manor, set in six hundred acres of Oxfordshire countryside, became the regular venue for gatherings of intellectuals and artists, and Lawrence seriously canvassed its potentialities as a location for his ideal colony, Rananim. Her husband was a Liberal MP who took an anti-war line in Parliament and was the spokesman in the House for a number of pacifist intellectuals, among whom Russell was the most notable. Lawrence and Russell planned a series of joint lectures on social reform and urgent contemporary issues. At this time Lawrence was an advocate of comprehensive nationalization and social security.

Early in March 1915, at his own suggestion, Lawrence paid a visit to Cambridge where he met, among others, the economist John Maynard Keynes and the philosopher G. E. Moore. He had already met at Greatham another prominent member of the Bloomsbury group, E. M. Forster, who had brought the disconcerting news that the police might take action against *The Prussian Officer*. The Cambridge visit was an utter failure on both sides, with Lawrence feeling revolted by the 'rottenness' and 'marsh stagnancy' of the life he saw. Lawrence and Russell, in spite of their apparent agreement on opposition to the war and the need for a social revolution, were intellectually and temperamentally utterly incompatible. Their association ended after a year or so in bitter hostility on both sides.

The horror of war and the impossibility of an early end to it were beginning to take an increasing toll of Lawrence's energy and spirits. He had completed *The Rainbow* and intended to write a sequel using much material already written but not worked into the final draft. His agent had already made some minor alterations but his publishers wanted Lawrence to make more, which he refused to do except for two deletions. His adamant refusal to pay the costs of the divorce (which exceeded all his wealth at the time anyway) had

A picture sent by Lawrence to Viola Meynell, March 2, 1915, with the message: 'I have finished my Rainbow'.

brought the threat of legal proceedings and bankruptcy very close. Disillusionment with the Cambridge–Bloomsbury circle produced in him an almost hysterical revulsion against practically everybody, both individually and generally considered. He hated, on the one hand, 'the little swarming selves' of the people he met (though he retained a personal fondness for E. M. Forster) and on the other he allowed himself outbursts such as 'I would like to kill a million Germans – two millions.' It is important to stress that in its context such a remark shows not the current anti-German hysteria, which Lawrence never succumbed to, but a much wider and more intense desperation over humanity and its insane capacity for self-destruction.

To add to it all, Lawrence's health was worsening. In August the Lawrences left Greatham and took a house in the Vale of Health in Hampstead. Lawrence wrote a long essay called 'The Crown', setting forth some of his social and psychological speculations which was published in a short-lived periodical, *The Signature*, edited by Murry. While living at Hampstead, Lawrence witnessed the first Zeppelin raid on London, an experience he recreated unforgettably in *Kangaroo* written seven years later. His immediate reaction is given in a letter written at the time: 'So it is the end – our world is gone, and we are like dust in the air.'

But the war years were to bring the Lawrences far more mental suffering than they had yet undergone, and a good deal of physical distress too. *The Rainbow* was published at the end of September 1915. The reviewers were almost uniformly hostile, regarding the novel as vicious and pornographic; one of them even wondered whether the publishers had actually read the book before publishing it. Within three weeks of publication, Scotland Yard officers had seized a thousand copies of the book with the full, not to say obsequious, cooperation of the publishers. Lady Ottoline's husband, Philip Morrell, was to ask a question about the matter in the Commons and Lawrence decided to wait and fight the prosecution, which was scheduled for mid-November. In the meantime he planned to found his ideal colony in Florida, not realizing at first that he would be unable to leave England without exemption from military service. Frieda's German birth was an obstacle in the matter of obtaining passports which Lady Cynthia's influence apparently helped to overcome.

At the trial the publishers apologized for having published *The Rainbow* which a witness for the prosecution described as 'a mass of obscenity of thought, idea and action throughout'. 'Methuen published the book and he almost wept before the magistrate,' according to Lawrence writing many years later. The magistrate made the point that the book should have been withdrawn after the unfavourable reviews and duly ordered the destruction of all copies seized. It seems probable that Lawrence's novel, though officially prosecuted for obscenity alone, was also considered an impediment to the recruiting campaign, especially at a time when the British military effort was going badly. The author's, and to some extent the central character's, anti-war sentiments were quite pronounced. This at any rate was Richard Aldington's view and he claimed Lawrence's authority for it.

The suppression of *The Rainbow* seriously diminished Lawrence's prospects of earning a living by writing. There was a certain amount of private support for him among intellectuals, especially the Bloomsbury group, but it led to no positive concerted action. Lawrence had received various sums of money for the Rananim enterprise, including £5 from Bernard Shaw and an anonymous gift (later returned) from Arnold Bennett. Among those who were briefly interested in the scheme was the young Aldous Huxley, who first met Lawrence at this time and thought him a good and even a great man. But the Florida plan crumbled, partly because the composer Frederick Delius, on whose orange plantation the colony was to be sited, was unenthusiastic. After a brief visit at Christmas to his two sisters, Lawrence and Frieda left for Cornwall, where Middleton Murry had arranged that they should have a loan of a house at Porthcothan near Padstow belonging to the novelist J. D. Beresford. They were to live in various parts of Cornwall for most of the next two years, undergoing the kind of experience which cumulatively Lawrence was to dramatize without much exaggeration as the 'Nightmare' chapter in *Kangaroo*.

In that book too is the account of the humiliating examination and rejection for military service, an experience Lawrence suffered on no less than three occasions. The first of these took place at Bodmin in June 1916, throughout the whole of which year the Lawrences lived in different parts of Cornwall. They left Beresford's cottage in February and after a brief stay in an inn rented a cottage in Higher Tregerthen, not far from St Ives. Lawrence was again ill that winter and spent his time correcting the proofs of his Italian travel book and getting together a volume of poems, *Amores*. The Murrys were persuaded by Lawrence to leave the cottage where they were living in the south of France and join the Lawrences in Cornwall, but the experience was not a satisfying one for either couple. There were frequent and fierce quarrels between Lawrence and Frieda, though they were always reconciled in apparent amity after each one. The friendship with Russell came to an end and that with Lady Ottoline became strained.

It was at this time that Lawrence began work on *Women in Love* as a separate novel. The bleak and wind-bitten Cornish landscape – 'a bare, forgotten country that doesn't belong to England' – suited his mood. With the spring his health improved and he found himself, in spite of everything, at peace with his surroundings and in the depths of his own self. The new book was going well. 'I have got a long way with my novel. It comes rapidly and is very good. When one is shaken to the very depths one finds reality in the unreal world. At present my real world is the world of my inner soul, which reflects on the novel I write. The outer world is there to be endured, it is not real – neither the outer life.' This is how Lawrence wrote about himself and his new novel to Lady Ottoline, who was to appear unflatteringly portrayed as Hermione Roddice in it. By August he had definitely settled on the title *Women in Love* and by September the book was finished, though it was not published till 1920.

The pressures of the outer world could not be shaken off as easily as Lawrence would have wished. With many of his friendships broken or near breaking point (the final break with Lady Ottoline was to come when she realized how she had been depicted in the new novel), Lawrence again tried to get visas for America, especially as there was no prospect of English publication for the new novel. The only book by him to be published in 1917 was the collection of poems dealing with the conflicting relationship between Frieda and himself, at various times called 'Poems of a Married Man' and 'Man and Woman' and finally published as *Look! We Have Come Through!* American visas were refused, and after brief visits to friends in Berkshire and his sister in Derbyshire, Lawrence returned to Cornwall where Frieda was now ill.

In June 1917 Lawrence was again asked to report for medical examination at Bodmin. Meanwhile, the fact that Frieda was a German and was receiving letters from abroad was arousing increasing local suspicion about the couple in a region never notable for its acceptance of strangers. Lawrence and Frieda were almost constantly spied on, indoors and out. Things came to a head one evening when they visited Bosigran Castle, then occupied by their friend Cecil Gray. A loose blind flapping in the wind in a lighted room resulted in accusations that they were sending secret messages to enemy submarines (the window overlooked a stretch of ocean where there was considerable naval activity). On 12 October, police entered the Lawrences' cottage (which they had turned upside down the day before) and ordered them to leave Cornwall within three days and report to the police of the area they moved to. Lawrence wrote to Cynthia Asquith: 'we're as innocent . . . as the rabbits in the field outside' – and added, 'It is all very sickening, and makes me weary'.

Through Lady Cynthia's influence he hoped to return to Cornwall before the end of the year. In the meantime they moved to Hampstead and then to the London flat shared by Richard Aldington (then away at the front) and H. D. Though the Cornish authorities had asked the Lawrences to report to the local police, the London police, did not seem to have heard of them, a fact which later caused Lawrence some sardonic amusement. But he found that 'London is really very bad: gone mad, in fact . . . people are not people any more: they are factors, really ghastly, like lemures, evil spirits of the dead'. In London, Lawrence began to write *Aaron's Rod* which contains satirical portraits of most of the people he knew at this time, including himself. He told Lady Cynthia he 'fell in hate' with people as others fell in love.

The anti-humanity which is such a powerful current of feeling in *Women in Love* was building up within him. The double blow of the suppression of *The Rainbow* and the expulsion from Cornwall was aggravated by the disappointment over the Rananim enterprise, to which Lawrence still stubbornly clung and whose locale had now shifted in his mind to South America, together with some change of personnel. Coming so close together, these experiences scarred him for life, both as writer and man. In her autobiography Frieda wrote: 'when we were turned out of Cornwall something changed in Lawrence for ever'.

After a short stay in Berkshire again, the couple now moved to a cottage which Lawrence's sister Ada had found them in the Derbyshire hills, near Matlock. The American poet Amy Lowell had given him £60 the previous November and he had received small sums from one or two others. This was all the money he had in the world till he received a grant of £50 from the Royal Literary Fund. In addition to working on *Aaron's Rod*, he was also preparing essays on American literature for possible publication in the United States. Some of them were eventually published in *The English Review* in 1918–19 and they appeared in book form, revised and enlarged as *Studies in Classic American Literature* in 1922. While in Derbyshire he was visited by a man who worked for the Oxford University Press and was commissioned to write a school text book on European history, in preparation for which he read avidly and copiously, particularly Gibbon and Carlyle. The book was not published till 1921 and even then *Movements in European History* appeared under the pseudonym Lawrence H. Davison. It is one of the least known and most undervalued of Lawrence's books and often has the vividness and urgency of the novels and travel writings.

On his thirty-third birthday Lawrence received an official letter requiring him to attend his third military medical examination, the worst ordeal so far. Once again he was classified as unfit for military service. Less than two months later on November 11, the war ended and Lawrence tried unsuccessfully to get a job in the Ministry of Education. He was also asked to contribute some essays to *The Times Educational Supplement*, but these were rejected. He continued working on the history text book and completed a play, *Touch and Go*.

David Garnett recalls meeting Lawrence at a party in London on Armistice night. 'He looked ill and unhappy, with no trace of that gay and sparkling love of life in his eyes which had been his most attractive feature six years before.' Amid all the rejoicing Lawrence uttered a sombre warning that the war was not really over, that the hate and the evil were greater than ever before, that Germany would soon rise up again and that Europe, and especially England, was done for.

The years of exile: Sicily, Australia, New Mexico

In the last chapter of *Aaron's Rod*, Rawdon Lilly, who speaks for the author, says: 'there are only two great dynamic urges in *life:* love and power.' Lawrence's attention as a novelist was shifting from the first of these to the second, though he returned to the 'love urge' in his last novel, *Lady Chatterley's Lover.* His political views at this time amounted to a sort of guild socialism, but he was increasingly preoccupied with the problem of political authority and his wartime experiences had made him deeply mistrustful of the working of democracy. The notion of a broadly socialist economic system was uneasily allied with the emerging idea of the saviour-hero, the natural leader whom the people will inevitably recognize and obey.

Lawrence's health was bad, but his financial state had improved. *New Poems* was published in October 1918 by Martin Secker, who remained Lawrence's main English publisher throughout the writer's life. He had received payment for some contributions to magazines and £50 for the history text book. In March of the new year Edward Marsh also sent him £20 from the Rupert Brooke memorial fund. The determination to leave England was as steadfast as ever but in the first few months of 1919 Lawrence was too ill to travel. His relations with Frieda were also going through a stormy phase. When she went to Germany he did not go with her. For a brief period he considered the possibility of going to Palestine with the psychoanalyst David Eder. Amy Lowell had persuaded Lawrence to defer his trip to the United States. Eventually Lawrence made a voyage, bound for Italy.

He made his way to Florence where Frieda was to meet him, but she was delayed and Lawrence stayed there for three weeks. There he met Norman Douglas, writer and bon viveur (who had met Lawrence shortly after *The White Peacock* was published), and through him a Maltese with a shadowy past called Maurice Magnus. Magnus committed suicide not long afterwards and Lawrence wrote a long introduction, one of his finest non-fictional prose writings, to his *Memoirs of the Foreign Legion.* From Florence he travelled to Rome and Capri where he met Compton Mackenzie and Mary Cannan, both of whom he had first met in his Chesham days. At Capri he also met the novelist Francis Brett Young who thought Lawrence a 'timid, shrinking, sensitive, violent, boastful, brazen creature'. For his part Lawrence thought Capri 'a stewpot of semi-literary cats'. In late February he crossed to Sicily and rented the upper floor of an old farm-house in Taormina, on a hill looking out to the blue sea and snow-covered Etna. 'Lovely, lovely Sicily,' he wrote in the Introduction to Magnus' *Memoirs*; 'the dawnplace, Europe's dawn, with Odysseus pushing his ship out of the shadows into the blue. Whatever had died for me, Sicily had not then died; dawn-lovely Sicily, and the Ionian Sea.'

Frieda joined him in Taormina and they made a brief visit to Malta. Lawrence continued with *Aaron's Rod*, as well as resuming work on *The Lost Girl*, begun before the war in 1913, the manuscript of which Else Jaffe now sent him. When Frieda went back to Germany, Lawrence returned to Italy, staying in a villa in San Gervasio, near Florence. Mussolini's Fascists were much in evidence at this time and Lawrence saw scenes of rioting and violence which he alludes to in his prose writings as well as in some of the poems written at this time, later collected as *Birds, Beasts and Flowers*. He and Frieda met again in Florence. Their need of each other remained greater than the differences between them throughout their life together.

Early in 1921 they went on a fortnight's excursion to Sardinia and less than two months later Lawrence had finished writing *Sea and Sardinia*. The capacity to capture the spirit of places which he visited only for very brief spells was one of Lawrence's particular gifts, and finds expression not only in his formal writing but in the letters he wrote from all over the world. Norman Douglas found him writing an essay on Florence almost as soon as he arrived in the city.

In April Frieda went back to Germany as her mother was ill and Lawrence this time decided to revisit the country which, since the end of the war, he had been disinclined to do. He joined Frieda and her mother, who came to grow very fond of Lawrence, at Ebersteinberg, near Baden. Here he completed *Aaron's Rod* and the first draft of *Fantasia of the Unconscious*, a sequel to his *Psychoanalysis and the Unconscious* which had recently appeared in America. That summer the Lawrences stayed with Frieda's younger sister Johanna (Nusch) in Thumersbach in the Austrian Alps. It was Johanna's marriage and the Alpine setting of their home which Lawrence used for the short story 'The Captain's Doll' written later that year. Meanwhile Secker published both *The Lost Girl* and *Women in Love*, which had been badly received. Lawrence was threatened with legal proceedings by Philip Heseltine (Peter Warlock) who considered himself libelled in the figure of Halliday in the novel.

Altogether Lawrence spent two years in Taormina. He was on the point of accepting an invitation from an American admirer, Mabel Dodge Sterne, to visit New Mexico at the beginning of 1922. Instead he decided at the last minute to go to Ceylon to join two other American friends he had met in Capri, Earl and Achsah Brewster who had gone there to study Buddhism. On the first day of their arrival there, they were so taken by the beauty of the island that Frieda exclaimed that it was the loveliest spot on earth, while Lawrence said 'I shall never leave it'. But he found more than the heat oppressive. 'I feel the East is not for me', he wrote. 'It seems to me the life drains away from one here. ... One could quite easily sink into a kind of apathy, like a lotus on a muddy pond, indifferent to anything.' After six weeks Lawrence's restlessness led him to take ship for Australia with no clear idea of why he was going or what he would do when he got there. On the voyage he spent his time translating the Sicilian novelist Giovanni Verga. 'Don't know what we'll do in Australia – don't care. The world of idea may be all alike, but the world of physical feeling is very different – one suffers getting adjusted – but that is part of the adventure.'

They spent less than three months in Australia before sailing on to San Francisco, bound for the artists' colony over which the wealthy and much divorced Mabel Sterne was presiding. But during seven weeks of his stay in a house by the Pacific near the small mining town of Thirroul, Lawrence began the novel *Kangaroo* and finished all of it except the last chapter, which was written at Taos. He also revised a novel called *The Boy in the Bush* by the Australian woman novelist M. L. Skinner. (The name of the house in Thirroul was 'Wywurk'.) Of all Lawrence's novels *Kangaroo* is the one least concerned with formal coherence. The main narrative, such as it is, is interrupted half way through by the 'Nightmare' chapter, undeniably powerful but only tenuously connected to the main theme. There are other digressions (significantly, one chapter is entitled 'Bits') mainly culled from Australian newspapers Lawrence was reading at the time, from which he also took details about Australian union organization and other matters for the story proper, which is resumed and concluded rather abruptly. While *Kangaroo* may be important for understanding Lawrence's abstract political and social ideas at the time, his imaginative energies are engaged almost entirely by the autobiographical narrative of his wartime experiences in London and Cornwall and by his response to the Australian landscape. His main impression of Australia was of the contrast between the immense primeval emptiness of the land and the almost accidental and irrelevant presence on it of human, especially European, life: 'Australia is a weird, big country. It feels so empty and untrodden ... even Sydney, which is huge, begins to feel unreal ... as if life here really had never entered in: as if it were just sprinkled over, and the land lay untouched.'

Mabel Sterne (who had left her third husband and was now living with her Red Indian chauffeur Tony Luhan) had built a little white adobe house for the Lawrences to live in. (Lawrence later said that adobe was his favourite building material because of its impermanence.) But before they could settle there they were whisked off at Mabel's insistence to witness an Apache fiesta more than one hundred miles away, a visit described in 'Indians and an Englishman'.

By now Lawrence was as well known in America as in Europe (his American publisher Thomas Seltzer visited him in Taos) and he found the visits from artists and intellectuals at Taos a distraction. The Lawrences therefore moved to an abandoned ranch some distance away, lent them by Mabel Luhan. Two Danish artists, Knud Merrild and Kai Gotzsche, helped them to get the ranch ready and have recorded, as Lawrence himself has, his intense and abiding pleasure in ordinary physical tasks such as woodwork, painting and making bread.

Relations between Mabel and Frieda were never cordial and Lawrence too showed his impatience with the somewhat domineering Mabel, as he did with nearly everyone with whom he had close and prolonged contact. (According to one visitor, Lawrence once suggested that his hostess should be tarred and feathered and railroaded out of Taos.) It was not the expatriates he met who engaged his attention in New Mexico any more than in Italy. It was the sense of a different, more primitive and deeper level of life, superficially affected but essentially untouched by European religion and culture, which he instinctively felt among the Pueblo Indians. This feeling for the primitive had always been an element of Lawrence's outlook on life, but it found its sharpest expression during his period in New Mexico. He associated this deeper level of existence with the sweep and grandeur of the landscape itself through which he felt the pulse of a religion which made Christianity and even Buddhism seem shallow and unreal by comparison. In his essay 'New Mexico', posthumously published in *Phoenix*, he described both the impact of the new land and its difference from his travel experiences so far: 'New Mexico . . . liberated me from the present era of civilization, the great era of material and mechanical development. Months spent in holy Kandy, in Ceylon, the holy of holies of southern Buddhism had not touched the great psyche of materialism and idealism which dominated me. And years, even in the exquisite beauty of Sicily . . . had not shattered the essential Christianity on which my character was established. Australia was a sort of dream or trance . . . But the moment I saw the brilliant, proud morning shine high up over the deserts of Santa Fé, something stood still in my soul, and I started to attend.'

The novel in which Lawrence crystallized his response to the new territory and its culture was written in less than six weeks and was originally called *Quetzalcoatl* (though it is possible that this draft, which has survived, is not complete). It was written not in Taos (which Lawrence was beginning to find unbearable) but at the lakeside village of Chapala, thirty-five miles from Guadalajara in Mexico. Here the Lawrences settled after six months in Taos and a short period in Mexico City in between. Beneath the surface disturbance of political factions – socialist, communist, fascist – Lawrence sensed in Mexico the dark, enduring passivity of Indian life and believed it had in it the seeds of a new and different growth. His Mexican novel finally emerged as *The Plumed Serpent* early in 1925. The writing of it drained him completely and he almost died of the illness to which he succumbed on the very day he finished the final version. It was the only original fiction he produced on his first American visit and from the beginning Lawrence insisted that it was the most important work he had written so far. The word 'important' appears in almost all his references to it at the time.

The Plumed Serpent opens with the description of a bullfight, based on one Lawrence had seen in Mexico City with some American friends until they could stand it no longer. For most readers this is one of the high-lights of the novel. In many ways *The Plumed Serpent* is the culmination of those speculations on the relation of political authority to individual fulfilment which had concerned Lawrence in *Aaron's Rod* and *Kangaroo*. In the first of these two novels Rawdon Lilly had expressed his conviction that the true centre of life which the European races had lost was to be found not among the Eastern people but in the Indians of South America: 'I would have loved the Aztecs and the Red Indians. I *know* they hold the element in life which I am looking for – they had living pride.' In *The Plumed Serpent* Lawrence works out the political implications of the view that true fulfilment in life comes not from the conflict of assertive wills – 'Bolshevism is one sort of bullying, capitalism is another' – but from each man recognizing 'the God of his manhood'. This in turn can only come about when a leader springs up whose appeal to men goes beyond narrow political and social considerations – 'the white anti-Christ of charity, and socialism, and politics, and reform' – which will only destroy Mexico, whose secret the ancient Incas, like all pagan peoples, had. Lawrence read a good many books on Mexican civilization in preparation for his novel, among them Prescott's *Conquest of Mexico*, Lewis Spence's *Gods of Mexico* and *Fundamental Principles of Old and New World Civilization* by Zelia Nuttall who appears as 'Mrs Norris' in *The Plumed Serpent*. But it was neither the past nor the present of Mexico considered in itself that interested Lawrence. The story of the inspired leader Don Ramon and his gospel of the return of Quetzalcoatl, the ancient bird-serpent god of wind and rain, is told chiefly in relation to its impact on Kate Leslie, the Irish woman whose scepticism gradually turns into acceptance of Don Ramon and the mysterious but quite palpable 'blood intimacy' that unites him to his followers far below the level of intellectual agreement. The new religion is implicitly and even quite explicitly presented as a necessary alternative to the rampant materialism of modern civilization and what Lawrence saw as the decayed Christianity which serves it and is served by it. Perhaps there is a faint unwitting irony in the fact that some of the hymns of the new religion which appear in the novel are based on those sung at the Congregational Chapel at Eastwood and half-remembered from childhood. Most readers, of whom I am one, find the incantatory rhetoric and prophetic stridency of *The Plumed Serpent* repellent, but it is pointless to condemn Lawrence for sacrificing artistry to preaching. By 1925, when the book was published, Lawrence certainly believed that the most urgent task of imaginative fiction was precisely to preach the gospel of a new heaven on earth. For better or worse *The Plumed Serpent* is a religious novel, in both the limiting and the liberating senses of the word.

Altogether Lawrence spent almost exactly three years in America, mainly in New Mexico and Mexico, leaving it for the last time in September 1925, when he was forty years old. During this period he visited several North American cities, including Los Angeles, Chicago and New York, which he disliked, finding Chicago 'more alive and more real'. In August 1923 Frieda had sailed to Europe but Lawrence stayed behind, a situation increasingly typical of their stormy relationship. Lawrence spent his time travelling in various parts of America and Mexico, correcting the proofs of *Kangaroo* and revising the manuscript of a novel by the Australian writer M. L. Skinner, later published as *The Boy in the Bush*. He was also preparing a new collection of poems, mainly written in Sicily, *Birds, Beasts and Flowers*, and working on the proofs of his translations of Giovanni Verga.

In December he was back in London and the damp and fog made his health worse while his spirits were sickened by what he thought of as the spiritual decay and intolerable provincialism of outlook of a once great nation. In his essay (written on his visit for the *Adelphi* magazine but rejected by its editor, Murry), Lawrence writes: 'In the small things of life the Englishman is the only perfect civilized being. But God save me from such civilization'; and went on, 'Look at us now. Not a man left inside all the millions of pairs of trousers.'

Lawrence felt, probably rightly, that he had sufficiently impressed Mabel Luhan with his ideas (although he could not tolerate her company for very long) to be able to found his ideal colony of Rananim in Taos. After spending Christmas with his sisters, he and Frieda travelled to Germany from where Lawrence wrote 'A Letter from Germany' with its prophetic vision of imminent catastrophe. They were back in London early in February 1925. Shortly after their arrival there occurred the notorious dinner party at the Cafe Royal in London of which vehement and varying accounts have been given by some of the participants (and at second hand by others). With so many versions to choose from, it is impossible to say exactly what was said and done, but the main outline is fairly clear. Several of Lawrence's literary and artistic acquaintances were there, including Mark Gertler, the Carswells and Murry. Lawrence, who like the rest had had a good deal to drink, invited all present to join him in founding Rananim at Taos, to which most of the guests agreed. Murry then kissed Lawrence, who embraced him and said: 'Don't betray me', to which Murry's reply was: 'I love you Lorenzo but I won't promise not to betray you.' According to Murry he said this because he did not know how long he could keep the secret of the love which had sprung up at this time between himself and Frieda. Koteliansky, one of the guests, broke most of the glasses during the evening, and shortly after the exchange Lawrence was sick on the tablecloth. Next morning he told Catherine Carswell that he had made a fool of himself, adding that it did not matter as long as one first admitted and then forgot it.

Among the company at the Cafe Royal was a deaf woman painter named Dorothy Brett, the daughter of Viscount Esher and an acquaintance of Lawrence's Garsington days. She was the only one who accompanied the Lawrences when they sailed to New York in March on their way to New Mexico.

At Taos Lawrence refused Mabel Luhan's offer of her son's ranch as a gift, but Frieda accepted it in exchange for the manuscript of *Sons and Lovers*. The ranch was high above the Lobo peak and there was a one-roomed cabin for Brett (as she liked to call herself). At Kiowa ranch Lawrence once more immersed himself delightedly in the simple daily round of household tasks, chopping wood, drawing water, cooking and cleaning. Here he wrote 'The Woman Who Rode Away', 'St Mawr' and 'The Princess'.

In the autumn of 1924 Lawrence's father died. They had never been close but towards the end of his life Lawrence felt he had been less than fair to his father, especially in *Sons and Lovers*. He thought he had let his mother's disappointment over her marriage blind him to the very real virtues of her husband.

In order to escape the sharp winter winds, the Lawrences, accompanied by Brett, moved southwards, first to Mexico City then to Oaxaca, where he revised *The Plumed Serpent*, completing it the following February. Here he also wrote some of the essays later included in *Mornings in Mexico* and an Epilogue to *Movements in European History*, which was not published till 1971. The sentiments and imagery he uses here are very close to those of *The Plumed Serpent*, as a brief extract will show: 'This is our job, then, our uncommon-sense: to recognize the spark of nobleness inside us, and let it make us. To recognize the spark of *noblesse* in one another, and add our sparks together, to a flame. And to recognize the men who have stars, not mere sparks of nobility in their souls, and to choose these for leaders.'

At Oaxaca Lawrence was ill with malaria and dysentery. In Mexico City he was diagnosed as having tuberculosis and warned not to attempt the journey to Europe which he had contemplated. They returned to Taos but when the Lawrences moved back to Kiowa

Lawrence's cottage at Kiowa Ranch, near Taos, New Mexico.
The house at Chapala, Mexico, where Lawrence began The Plumed
Serpent.

ranch, Brett did not accompany them as Frieda could not tolerate her presence. Brett made Taos her home for the rest of her life, wrote the more or less obligatory memoir of Lawrence and died in 1979. While convalescing, Lawrence wrote the play *David* as well as several essays, including 'Reflections on the Death of a Porcupine'. As it would have been dangerous for him to spend the winter in New Mexico, they left once more for Europe, travelling by sea from New York, and October 1925 saw the Lawrences once more in the cold and fog of England. Lawrence visited his sisters and saw the landscapes of his childhood once more. After seeing a few friends of pre-war days in London, they left to visit Frieda's mother in Baden before moving on to Spotorno, near Genoa. Here they rented a villa from the man who was to be Frieda's third husband twenty-five years later.

Europe once more : death in Vence

This was late in 1925, when Lawrence had less than five years to live. Frieda's daughters, now grown up, came to see them before the year was out and the visit provoked the writing of 'The Virgin and the Gipsy'. In 1926 *The Plumed Serpent* was published. Lawrence was now a famous writer though not a wealthy one and had almost as many fervent admirers as disgusted detractors. Reviewing *Kangaroo* two years earlier J. D. Beresford had 'to acknowledge without any qualification whatever that this is the work of genius, a thing separate in kind'.

When Lawrence's sister came to visit them, he was ill again, this time with influenza. He accompanied her on a week's trip to Monte Carlo, then visited his old American friends the Brewsters in Capri, where he met Brett once more. He visited friends in various parts of Italy before joining Frieda and her daughters in Florence. When the children returned to London, the Lawrences rented the Villa Mirenda at Scandicci, a few miles from Florence and within reach of the Etruscan ruins at Cerveteri, Tarquinia and Volterra which provided the material for *Etruscan Places*. They were in Baden for the seventy-fifth birthday of Frieda's mother and back in London for the last time in August 1926. He spent a holiday on the Lincolnshire coast with his sisters and paid his last visit to Eastwood. It was the year of the General Strike and the Eastwood miners were still out though the strike was officially over. Lawrence visited some of the scenes of his childhood with an old Eastwood friend, Willie Hopkin, who asked him when he would return. 'Never!' came the reply, 'I hate the damned place.'

Returning to Scandicci, Lawrence began writing the story that was to become *Lady Chatterley's Lover*. His two recent visits to the Midlands at a time of social and economic unrest obviously influenced both the theme and the choice of setting. In its first version *Lady Chatterley's Lover* was finished by March 1927 though Lawrence was quite convinced that no publisher would accept it. He also did several oil paintings at this time, having got some used canvases from Maria Huxley who paid a visit to Scandicci with her husband, Aldous.

When Frieda visited her mother again Lawrence stayed with the Brewsters near Amalfi and visited the Etruscan tombs. During this period he wrote the story 'The Escaped Cock' (later called 'The Man Who Died'), suggested by the sight of a toy rooster escaping from an egg in a shop window. He also wrote a second version of *Lady Chatterley's Lover* and some essays about the Tuscan countryside including the beautiful 'Flowery Tuscany'.

His play *David* was being given a restricted performance in London in May but Lawrence was too ill to attend. In June he visited the Huxleys who were staying at the coast in Forte dei Marmi and bathing in the sea made Lawrence's condition worse. He had several haemorrhages and made his way painfully to the Austrian Tyrol, not far from where he had stayed a few years earlier with Frieda's younger sister and her husband. From here they went to stay with Frieda's elder sister at Irschenhausen. Lawrence refused to enter a sanatorium for treatment. Italy was no longer the place of enchantment it had been during his first post-war sojourn and his thoughts were once more turning wistfully westwards towards Mexico. He rewrote *Lady Chatterley's Lover* once more and had it finished by January of the new year, 1928. At this time he considered calling it *Tenderness*.

Meantime, as he himself wrote, 'my cough goes raking on', and the Lawrences now moved to Les Diablerets in Switzerland, 'to get myself solider this year'. Here they met the Huxleys, Aldous and Julian, and their wives. With the help of Maria Huxley and Catherine Carswell in London, Lawrence prepared an expurgated typescript of *Lady Chatterley's Lover* for his London publisher who nevertheless rejected it. But Lawrence was making arrangements for the unexpurgated version to be printed in Italy by his friend the Italian publisher Pino Orioli and issued to subscribers.

On their return to Florence, Frieda's daughter Barbara arrived with the suggestion that Dorothy Warren, owner of a London gallery, might be interested in mounting an exhibition of Lawrence's paintings. Lawrence took up the idea at once, partly because he was beginning to find painting an enjoyable change from writing, partly because he wanted to raise the money to return to America. In May the Brewsters paid them a visit and were so distressed by Lawrence's wasted appearance that they insisted on going back to Switzerland with Frieda and him. They took a chalet at Gsteig-bei-Gstaad where Lawrence, in spite of his worsening condition, was busy handling the private distribution of *Lady Chatterley's Lover*, painting and writing newspaper articles (later collected as *Assorted Articles*). He also wrote some short stories, among them 'Blue Moccasins' and the later part of 'The Escaped Cock'.

Later that summer the Lawrences were the guests of Richard Aldington and his wife on the island of Port Cros near Toulon. Lawrence spent a disagreeable month here, gnawed by ill health, irritated by unfavourable reviews of his latest collection of stories, *The Woman Who Rode Away*, and nauseated by the negative outlook he discerned in Aldous Huxley's recently published *Point Counter Point* where Lawrence appears as Rampion. They spent the winter at Bandol on the mainland where, in addition to his other activities, the ailing Lawrence prepared a volume of short poems, penseés or *Pansies*.

Before it could be published, the manuscript of *Pansies* was seized in transit on the orders of the Home Secretary and submitted to the Director of Public Prosecutions, together with some copies of *Lady Chatterley's Lover* and another manuscript, the long Introduction Lawrence wrote for an American edition of his paintings. When *Pansies* eventually appeared in England the following summer, fourteen poems were left out, but the publicity arising from the seizure (questions were asked in Parliament as to who exactly authorized the confiscation) resulted in large profits from an unexpurgated edition published by an Australian friend of Lawrence on the Continent.

Lawrence was staying with the Huxleys at Forte dei Marmi when the exhibition of his paintings opened in London in June 1929. Several thousand people visited it during the first three weeks and some pictures had been sold. On July 5 the police raided the gallery, acting apparently on complaints from members of the public, and took away thirteen pictures, together with copies of a volume in which some of Lawrence's paintings were reproduced and a book of drawings by the German artist George Grosz, later to be banned by Hitler. They were persuaded to leave some Blake reproductions alone after being assured that the artist had been safely dead for over a century. The gallery continued with the exhibition but Lawrence advised closure as otherwise the seized paintings were in danger of being burnt. 'There is something sacred to me about my pictures,' Lawrence wrote to Dorothy Warren, owner of the gallery, 'and I will not have them burnt, for all the liberty of England. I am an Englishman, and I do my bit for the liberty of England. But I am most of all a man, and my first creed is that my manhood and my sincere utterance shall be inviolate and beyond nationality or any other limitation.'

In spite of opinions to the contrary expressed by eminent artists and art critics such as Augustus John and William Rothenstein (who were not called as witnesses at the official inquiry) an eighty-two-year old magistrate found Lawrence's paintings offensive, though they were

'Boccaccio Story' One of the oil paintings by Lawrence exhibited at the
Warren Gallery, London in June *1929* and seized by the police.

not actually declared obscene. They were allowed to be returned to the artist by the gallery after an assurance that they would not be exhibited. Lawrence's only public reaction was to spit out a few more savage little verses, some published as *Nettles* others as 'More Pansies' in the posthumous *Last Poems*.

The 'trial' of Lawrence's paintings took place in London in August 1929, when he had seven months more to live. Frieda had gone to London in June to see her children and visit the exhibition. Lawrence stayed with the Huxleys at Forte dei Marmi and went on to Florence in early July, where he heard the news about the exhibition. When the 'trial' began, he was in Baden with Frieda, visiting her aged mother with whom Lawrence did not get on during this visit. 'She would see me or anyone else die ten times over, to give her a bit more strength to drag on a few more meaningless years.' At the end of August Frieda and Lawrence left for Bavaria.

Lawrence was now a famous, even notorious author. Though never a wealthy man, he was now probably better off financially then he had ever been. His handling of the distribution of *Lady Chatterley's Lover* had proved lucrative, in spite of pirated editions and trouble with the censors. *Collected Poems* (which had appeared the previous year) and *Pansies* were selling well, and an unexpurgated version of the latter, privately printed, had sold out quickly. Up to the very end he continued to write. In addition to a pamphlet on 'Pornography and Obscenity' he now wrote the first version of one of his most beautiful poems, 'Bavarian Gentians', originally called 'Glory of Darkness' and suffused with intimations of mortality. He told the Brewsters that he had a feeling he would certainly die if he stayed in Germany. But five days before his last birthday he wrote to a friend from Bavaria: 'They say I can get well in quite a short time. I hope it's true – it may be really.'

He had been fairly comfortable in Bandol the previous winter, so they returned there once more, renting a small villa by the sea. Lawrence still responded with something like the old rapturous delight to the southern sun – 'I still love the Mediterranean, it still seems young as Odysseus, in the morning.' But his life was ebbing fast – 'I am so weak. And something inside me weeps black tears. I wish it would go away.'

In his last months he wrote 'A Propos of *Lady Chatterley's Lover*', an expanded version of the introduction to the Paris edition of the novel. Late in the year Frederick Carter, whose occult writings had interested Lawrence, came to Bandol to discuss his work and the possibility of having it published with an introduction by Lawrence. This 'introduction' grew into *Apocalypse*, published separately

Bust of Lawrence made during the last months of his life by the American sculptor Jo Davidson.

and posthumously, the last prose work Lawrence lived to complete. He also wrote some of his finest poems at this time, poems which have a tragic radiance, their vivid sense of life vibrant against the shadow of approaching death. Just three months before his own death news reached him of the suicide of an American friend, the poet Harry Crosby. 'That's all he could do with life, throw it away,' Lawrence exclaimed; 'how could he betray the great privilege of life?'

Lawrence himself never did. He had been in Bandol for nearly four months when early in the new year an English doctor who had heard from mutual friends in England about the seriousness of Lawrence's condition and was holidaying in France examined him. Lawrence was still hoping to return to New Mexico the following spring when Dr Morland found that he had been suffering from pulmonary tuberculosis for several years. He recommended complete rest in a sanatorium. Lawrence was reluctant but gave in after two weeks and was moved to a sanatorium at Vence above Nice. He had fewer visitors here than at Bandol, but they included the Huxleys and H. G. Wells. At Wells' suggestion the American sculptor Jo Davidson made a bust of Lawrence during his last days at Vence.

His sickness grew worse and Dr Morland diagnosed pleurisy. Lawrence insisted on leaving the sanatorium. A Corsican doctor who was called in said: 'He is living on his spirit.' He was moved to a rented villa. On the following day, he was in great pain and Huxley fetched a doctor who gave him a morphine injection. This eased the pain and the last words he is known to have uttered are: 'I am better now.' A little later he was breathing with difficulty and some time between ten and eleven o'clock on Sunday 2 March 1930 D. H. Lawrence died. He was buried at Vence and the ten mourners included the Huxleys and the poet Robert Nichols. An offer from the resident English chaplain to conduct an abbreviated service was declined. A headstone with a phoenix design – Lawrence's chosen emblem – was placed at the grave. Five years later his remains were cremated at Marseilles on Frieda's instructions and the ashes taken to Taos. Here they were mixed in with the cement used to make a small shrine to his memory at Kiowa ranch, because Frieda wished to make certain that the ashes could not be stolen.

Lawrence's grave at Vence. The stone was later removed to Eastwood and the ashes interred at Taos.

Lawrence's tomb at Kiowa ranch. Frieda's remains are interred at the entrance to the 'shrine'.

2   The intellectual background

The novelist as prophet

During the twenty or so years of his writing career Lawrence turned his hand to virtually every available literary form. Novels, short stories, poetry, plays, essays, travel books and reviews poured out from his prolific pen in a flood that ceased only with his death. In addition he was to the end an indefatigable letter writer and his letters rank with those of Keats and Hopkins as among the greatest in English. But Lawrence was and is clearly more, both in his own view and that of his readers then and now, than merely a literary man. There were other literary figures as celebrated as himself, some even more so – Bennett, Wells, Galsworthy, Kipling and others. But famous and widely read though they were (and some still are) none of them had the impact on their age and ours that Lawrence had. There is ample testimony to the sense of personal loss that people in many walks of life, some of whom had never set eyes on him, felt at his death. The words of the historian A. L. Rowse embody the feelings of innumerable others: 'D. H. Lawrence meant something special to the men of my generation: he was an essential part in our awakening to maturity. We saw something of life through his eyes: his mode of experience intimately affected ours.' And today, fifty years after Lawrence's death, later generations can echo Rowse's words: 'He was a part of me: he had entered into my veins at a very vulnerable moment, of adolescence changing into maturity. He was entwined in the fibres of my mind and heart. . . . '

It is possible that the novel was the form in which Lawrence made his most lasting contribution to English literature, though the long short story was a form in which he excelled and the quality and distinction of his poetry is being more and more widely recognized. Even the much neglected plays have been professionally performed with great success. But Lawrence, except at the very beginning, had no desire to be appraised in purely aesthetic terms. Once he had found his identity as a writer – and he did so very early – he insisted over and over again that the purpose of his writing was, in the last analysis, didactic. 'The purpose of art is moral,' he wrote, 'not aesthetic, not decorative, but moral.' And as a novelist, he considered himself 'superior to the poet, the philosopher and the saint' because the novel, by the vividness of its images of created life, could affect our moral sense below the level of mere intellect or opinion.

To his own generation and to ours Lawrence appears not only as an imaginative writer but as a distinct personality whose impact is quite palpable over and above his fictions, through them as well as apart from them. It is true, or almost true, as Aldous Huxley once remarked, that no one would have heard of a Lawrence who was not an artist. And Lawrence's own dictum, 'Never trust the artist, trust the tale', has been quoted *ad nauseam*, often against himself. But for better or worse, the artist is often inseparable from his work. This does not mean that the work must always be referred back to the life and only acquires value in so far as it illuminates that life, though Lawrence sometimes wrote as if this was true. In the Preface to his *Collected Poems*, for instance, he says: 'It seems to me that no poetry, not even the best, should be judged as if it existed in the absolute, in the vacuum of the absolute. Even the best poetry, when it is at all personal, needs the penumbra of its own time and place and circumstance to make it full and whole.' Perhaps there is an element of special pleading in that qualifying phrase 'when it is at all personal', as if Lawrence realized the exceptionally intimate relationship between his life, personality and work. It remains true that that relationship *is* intimate and that if we neglect it, under the influence of some notion of the 'impersonality of great art' or such like, we run the risk of misunderstanding Lawrence the artist as much as Lawrence the teacher. Even in the very best of his works, the two roles are never quite identical and their changing relationship is one of the most fascinating aspects of his work.

Throughout his work, in fiction and non-fiction, Lawrence challenged the received wisdom on a variety of topics – politics, psychology, education, religion, and of course sexual morality – and did not hesitate to express his own ideas, often not as an established and consistent body of counter arguments, but as a vehement critical exploration of existing ones. In nearly all his writing, even in his poetry, the need to 'air' his views, almost literally to give them room to breathe, is as urgent and compelling as any other. Many readers are repelled by what they consider Lawrence's tendency to preach, but it must be recognized that this tendency is integral, not accidental, to Lawrence the artist. Like Blake, Lawrence was a prophet, not in the vulgar sense of a foreteller of future events, but in the older Biblical sense of a crier forth of forgotten or unheeded truths.

It is possible that this prophetic strain in Lawrence was partly a result of his relation to the mainstream of literary and intellectual life in his day. Both his working class origin and his provincial background isolated him from the high culture of Edwardian and Georgian London. In a later section of this book I shall glance briefly at his strategy for gaining the attention of the arbiters of literary and cultural taste. But having gained their attention, he adopted the stance of the preacher and prophet in order to keep it, and the occasional stridency of his tone is an index both of his sense of the urgency and importance of what he had to say and his despair at ever getting enough people to listen and understand.

More specifically, Lawrence's first real contact with the world of ideas and vision in his own community at Eastwood would have been through a preacher, the Congregational minister, the Reverend Robert Reid, a close friend of Lawrence's mother. He was the founder of a literary society which met at the British School in Eastwood whose meetings were attended by Lawrence when he was still at school. It was he too, who by assisting Lawrence to become a pupil teacher, set his feet on the road that was to lead him out of both class and regional confinement. T. S. Eliot and others have belittled the value of this background, labelling it 'hymn-singing tin-chapel pietism', with the implication that it was the crudest form of revivalist religiosity. Other critics have perhaps overstated the opposite point of view and portrayed the young Lawrence as the heir to a vital and comprehensive tradition. Looking back, Lawrence himself offers a sane and balanced view of his religious upbringing. In 'Hymns in a Man's Life' he writes:

> I think it was good to be brought up a Protestant: and among Protestants, a Nonconformist, and among Nonconformists, a Congregationalist. Which sounds pharisaic. But I should have missed bitterly a direct knowledge of the Bible, and a direct relation to Galilee and Canaan, Moab and Kedron, those places that never existed on earth. . . . So, altogether, I am grateful to my 'Congregational' upbringing. The Congregationalists are the oldest Nonconformists, descendants of the Oliver Cromwell Independents. They still had a Puritan tradition of no ritual. But they avoided the personal emotionalism which one found among the Methodists when I was a boy.

It is clear that his Congregational background gave Lawrence at least two things of permanent importance. In the first place, and partly because of the stress his mother placed on regular religious activity, it focused his mind at an impressionable age on fundamental religious issues, leading to his early sceptical agnosticism and later to the very Lawrentian 'religion' of *The Plumed Serpent* and 'The Man Who Died'. And secondly, as the quotation above suggests, by impregnating his youthful consciousness with the language and rhythms of the Bible, it helped to form the staple of his prose style, as the psalms and hymns shaped the rhythm of his poetry. In another essay Lawrence writes:

> I was brought up on the Bible, and seem to have it in my bones. From early childhood I have been familiar with Apocalyptic language and Apocalyptic image: not because I spent my time reading Revelation, but because I was sent to Sunday School

and to chapel, to Band of Hope and to Christian Endeavour and was always having the Bible read to me.

Introduction to The Dragon of the Apocalypse, 1930.

No imaginative writer of the twentieth century shows so great an inwardness with the Bible as Lawrence; by comparison Shaw, who *knew* the Bible as well as Lawrence did, seems flashy and superficial in his use of it.

Lawrence and provincialism

The Congregational background links up with the other great centre of Lawrence's early education, Haggs Farm. The Lawrences and the Chambers' were both regular chapel-goers and it was this contact which led to Lawrence's first visit to the farm. It would be difficult to exaggerate the importance as a formative influence on Lawrence of his early years at Haggs Farm. All his life he remembered it as a place of almost paradisal delight. In one of the best of his early lyrics ('Renascence') he recalls the sights and sounds of the farm:

> And I woke to the sound of the wood-pigeon, and lay and listened
> Till I could borrow
> A few quick beats from a wood-pigeon's heart; and when I did rise
> Saw where the morning sun on the shaken iris glistened.
> And I knew that home, this valley, was wider than Paradise.

And less than two years before he died, he wrote to one of Jessie Chambers' brothers: 'Whatever I forget, I shall never forget the Haggs – I loved it so. I loved to come to you all, it really was a new life began in me there. ...' Part of this is of course the exile's sentimental nostalgia for home and the grown man's for lost childhood. But there is a good deal more than sentimentality of whatever kind involved. The Haggs offered, to begin with, not only a relief from the incessant quarrels between the parents, but a refuge from the grey and grimy squalor of Eastwood. True, the house in which Lawrence spent most of his childhood looked out on open country, but there is a notable difference between looking at the country and knowing oneself to be a part of its life. At Haggs, where he was soon regarded as one of the family, Lawrence could and did feel a part of the small farm and its life. Here he first experienced that delight in physical tasks which never left him all his life and which he celebrated so lyrically in *The White Peacock*, the more lyrically perhaps because he was only intermittently involved in it. Here too his intuitive almost subcutaneous awareness of nature and non-human life was stimulated and developed. Among the fields and woods in and around Haggs Lawrence came into living touch with the English countryside. That this is no sentimental figure of speech is shown repeatedly by the testimony of those who knew him

Haggs Farm, the Willey Farm of Sons and Lovers. 'And I knew that home, this valley, was wider than Paradise.'

at the time. In a memoir of Lawrence, J. D. Chambers (Jessie's brother) remembers that Lawrence 'came to the fields and woods at Haggs as into a new world, a species of fairy land, where the contact with nature was direct and free; where a robin building in an old kettle, a lark in a beast's hoofmark left in the stiff clay, and above all the white embroidery of lady smocks and the foam of bluebells over the wood in spring were a matter of perpetual wonder and genuine excitement. I have seen these things since, but never with the same thrill as when Bert was there to see them. He imparted some of his own intensity of living to the rest of us.' It was his experience of Haggs Farm that justified Lawrence saying in later life that the England he knew as a child was still 'the old agricultural England of Shakespeare and Milton and Fielding and George Eliot'. Perhaps his vision of the ideal colony of Rananim itself was shaped in part by those early memories of days at the farm. Most important of all, it was there that he met Jessie Chambers, the 'Miriam' of *Sons and Lovers*. Quite apart from the part she played in his emotional development, the influence of Jessie Chambers on Lawrence's intellectual growth was crucial. Though his mother certainly encouraged his literary interests, that encouragement had a quite practical intent, that her son should for ever escape the darkness of the mines by way of good, respectable 'daylight' employment. The intellectual limits of Mrs Lawrence's encouragement were set by her unwavering orthodox Congregationalism. It was through Jessie that Lawrence was able, intellectually at least, to break away from the constricting range of his mother's vision and to embark on those 'thought-adventures' whose meaning and value his mother would not even have understood had she lived, let alone appreciated. (She even disapproved of the direction her son took in an early version of *The White Peacock*.) Though Jessie was never the dominant partner in their relationship, it was in the glow of his new friendship that Lawrence set out on a prodigious programme of reading and discussion far surpassing that which most youths of his age were (or are) getting at more formal centres of education. It is not merely the sheer quantity and range of books which they read together that is astonishing; it is also the depth and intensity with which they responded to what they read. To these young people reading was not a pastime but a passion; in a very real sense they read as if their life depended upon it. Under Lawrence's guidance they read together virtually all the great writers in English and a good many of the lesser ones, and the process continued while Lawrence underwent training at University College, but it was begun much earlier. Jessie Chambers has said that at one time or another Lawrence read out aloud to her almost every poem in *The Golden Treasury*. The emotional element in their friendship obviously coloured both the choice and interpretation of a good deal of what they read; it is quite clear, for instance, that Lawrence's fondness for Meredith's poetry, especially 'Love in the Valley', was due partly to a sense of close identification between his own situation and that of the poem. More poignantly, we learn how one Christmas vacation Lawrence insisted on their reading *Coriolanus* together and remarked at the end to Jessie: 'You see, it's the mother who counts, the wife hardly at all. The mother is everything to him.'

Nor was their reading confined to imaginative literature. Among the philosophers they read were Schopenhauer and Spinoza, Mill, Spencer, Ernest Haeckel and the British empirical philosophers. Here another important intellectual centre in Lawrence's early life ought also to be mentioned, namely the friendship formed early and lasting right through to the end of Lawrence's life, between himself and William Hopkin, a local councillor at Eastwood and a life-long socialist. Lawrence was a frequent visitor at the Hopkins' house where he had the opportunity to meet personally or learn of the views of such radical figures as Ramsay MacDonald and Edward Carpenter. Though in those days he never took any active part in politics, he was deeply interested in radical political views and associated ideas regarding women's emancipation and some of these, greatly modified, remained with him throughout his life.

Without belittling the value of what he received from his two years at Nottingham University College, it may be fairly said that it was at Eastwood and especially at Haggs that the foundations of Lawrence's intellectual development were laid – or rather, that is where he first laid them himself. The questing spirit which even his earliest schoolmaster remembered in Lawrence was strengthened and reinforced in discussions first with Jessie and the Hopkin circle, and then among the group of friends, all more or less the same age, who called themselves the Pagans. Some of these discussions, if we are to take *The White Peacock* as documentary evidence, may have been callow and self-publicizing, as many in formal academic circles often are. But in general, Jessie Chambers' memoir is only one testimony out of many to the fact that in those early years Lawrence was in contact with and contributed to a rich and varied intellectual community. His propensity to dominate whatever group he was part of is also well documented. In the picture of the young Lawrence passionately pronouncing his views on religion, sex and art to a group of fascinated listeners of his own generation, their scepticism invariably overcome by the sheer hypnotic spell of his personality, we may see in little a version of what Lawrence the writer was to become to his readers – a prophet who convinced few but captivated nearly all by the power and passion of his insights. The idea that the lack of an Oxbridge education turned Lawrence into some sort of intellectually deprived urchin pathetically attempting to cover his nakedness with a few shreds and patches filched from whatever lay to hand and put together as best he could is as ludicrously inapplicable to Lawrence as it was to Hardy or George Eliot.

Lawrence and provincialism: the example of Hardy

Mention of Hardy and George Eliot leads quite naturally to a consideration of Lawrence's relation to his native landscape on the one hand and on the other to his reception by the literary establishment of metropolitan England. Lawrence is not, of course, a regional novelist in any limiting sense any more than are either of the other novelists named. But, like that of Hardy and Eliot, most of his work has a deep and vital relation to a part of England which, until very recently, tended to be regarded either as Matthew Arnold regarded it, a region of outer darkness beyond the pale of high culture or, condescendingly, as quaintly 'provincial'.

While the affinities between Lawrence's situation, and those of the two older writers and the positive aspects of 'provincialism' need stressing, we need also to take note of the differences of geography and generation. Hardy's Dorset was in many ways quite unlike Lawrence's Nottinghamshire. In Hardy's childhood, that part of England was virtually isolated from the rest of the country, more deeply set in the old ways of life and thought, less exposed to the inroads of progress. As a child Hardy remembered the coming of the railways. When Lawrence was born the railways had already been in the district for half a century. Hardy documents the tragedy of rural decay, Lawrence that of industrial dehumanization. While there were no mines in Eastwood itself it was in the heart of the mining country and its impact was as palpable as the ubiquitous soot. Though he never went down a mine himself, Lawrence's youth was spent very close to the life of the mining community in every sense. One of the painful memories of his childhood, vividly recalled in *Sons and Lovers*, was the weekly ordeal of collecting his father's wages from the colliery office. The pattern of the miners' life, with its extrovert masculinity centred upon the coal-face and the pub he knew at one remove; but the daily impact of the miner, a creature of underground darkness with something of an earth-spirit about him as he surfaced into the shabby genteel home life – that Lawrence not only knew at first hand but returned to throughout his writing. Finally, Lawrence was not rooted in the past of his native landscape in the way Hardy was. The constant moving from one home to another in childhood is representative of his equivocal relation to his home village, as is the fact that Eastwood was not the native place of either his father or his mother. Lawrence did not have Hardy's deep and abiding curiosity about his ancestors, nor did he have any cause to do so; the provincial inheritance came to him through other sources – Haggs Farm, the Congregational chapel, the library, his mother's gentility and his father's zest. Yet the links with Hardy are as obvious as they are important. It is not mere coincidence that Hardy was the only author to whom Lawrence devoted a full-length study.

Lawrence is closer geographically to George Eliot than to Hardy, but here too the differences are important. The 'country of my heart', as Lawrence called it, the Derbyshire–Nottinghamshire border country, is neither very far nor very different from George Eliot's Warwickshire. It is not surprising that *The Mill on the Floss* was a book which the young Lawrence read with sympathy and delight. But Eastwood was obviously not the centre of an agricultural–mercantile community such as George Eliot often depicted, nor did Lawrence have her acquaintance with rural landed gentry (her father was bailiff to a great landowner). The provincial mine-owning plutocrats who served as a model for the Criches in *Women in Love* were a very different matter, and in his early work up to *Sons and Lovers* they appear only marginally and seen from the outside. By the time he came to write *Women in Love*, however, he was acquainted with this class at close quarters.

Recalling such specific differences makes it easier to see Lawrence's distinctive place within the provincial tradition and his distinctive contribution to it, for no significant figure passively occupies a 'place' in a tradition without enlarging it. Something has already been said of the intellectual life of the community into which Lawrence was born, one that has many affinities with that of the young George Eliot. It may be said that in novels such as *Sons and Lovers* and to a far greater extent *Lady Chatterley's Lover* Lawrence is registering an imaginative response to the same movements of social change in roughly the same part of England as George Eliot, but a century later. In *The Rainbow* he takes a panoramic view of the process by cutting into a sweep of time that takes him back to George Eliot's day. As Lawrence himself wrote, he grew up 'in this queer jumble of the old England and the new'. The old was represented by the still open countryside where his father could catch rabbits as he set off at first light across the dewy fields for a day's work at the coal face. The mines themselves were the new, though Lawrence is careful to point out that 'the pit did not mechanize men'. The butty system under which the miners of Lawrence's father's generation worked did not have the faceless impersonality which came at a later stage of mechanization. The figure of the miner still unbroken in spirit either by the genteel pressures of his 'superior' wife or by the dead weight of industrialization, still sensitive to the subtler springs of life and beauty underneath the grime and coarseness is one of the archetypes of Lawrentian fiction. It is at least as important a legacy of his regional background as any other. The process of change, from a more human pattern of work to a dehumanized one and its effects on the human beings involved, is illustrated at one end of the social-economic scale by the contrast between Gerald Crich, the new industrial capitalist with his worship of productivity and efficiency, and the older, paternalistic and finally defeated figure of his father. At the other end, we see its eroding effects in the gradual diminution of Walter Morel in *Sons and Lovers* who is undefeated but whose energies are sapped by the unceasing struggle. Lawrence pinpointed the generation of miners of his own age-group as the first to be 'tamed' by their women who, defeated in their struggle against their husbands, realized in their sons their ideals of respectability, sobriety and 'getting on' in life:

> The women almost invariably nagged about material things ...
> It was a mother's business to see that her sons 'got on', and it was the man's business to provide the money. In my father's generation, with the old, wild England behind them, and the lack of education, the man was not beaten down. But in my generation, the boys I went to school with, colliers now, have all been beaten down, what with the din-din-dinning of Board Schools, books, cinemas, clergymen, the whole national human consciousness hammering on the fact of material prosperity above all things.
>
> 'Nottingham and the Mining Countryside'.

In his writings as in his life Lawrence always tried to balance these two aspects of his provincial legacy, the 'education' which, whatever its limitations, enabled him to escape from the constricting future that Eastwood offered, and that fierce independence of spirit·which he came more and more to associate with his father. In a passage such as the one quoted, we see Lawrence outlining the territory he himself explored in the novels, unknown in George Eliot's day and only dimly prefigured in part of *Jude the Obscure*.

Lawrence's relation to Hardy is as intimate as it is problematic. The superficial similarities – the feeling for landscape, the sense of an England far removed from the genteel south, the intimations of tragic scope in the fates of ordinary people, do not quite account for Lawrence's increasing awareness that Hardy, rather than George Eliot, was the writer whose themes and outlook pointed the way forward for him (though when he began his first novel he decided to use George Eliot's formal pattern and 'begin with two couples'). The immediate impetus behind his long *Study of Thomas Hardy* was sheer frustration and despair over the war: 'What colossal idiocy, this war,' Lawrence wrote in a letter a few months after its outbreak; 'out of sheer rage I've begun my book about Thomas Hardy.' The idea of the book had occurred to him some time before the war began. He started writing it in September 1914 and completed it before the end of the year. 'It will be about anything but Thomas Hardy,' the letter quoted above continues and this is true enough about the

Study as it stands, but what is equally significant is that, however idiosyncratic his criticism of Hardy may be, he needed the work and example of the older novelist to focus his speculations on a vast array of topics – love, war, power, mental and non-mental consciousness, male and female, and a host of others. And he felt too that his own genius lay in the further exploration of the form of the 'poetic novel' of which Hardy was a pioneer rather than in the more naturalistic modes of nineteenth century fiction.

Lawrence's comments on Hardy's characters in Chapter III of the *Study* indicates the kind of interest he has in them, an interest very much that of the creative novelist aware of similar objections that might be raised against his own work. They foreshadow the fully developed Lawrentian view of character formulated in the famous letter to Edward Garnett which will be discussed later. 'One thing about them,' Lawrence writes about Hardy's characters, 'is that none of the heroes and heroines care very much for money or immediate self-preservation and all of them are struggling hard to come into being. What exactly the struggle into being consists of, is the question. But most obviously, from the Wessex novels, the first and chiefest factor is the struggle into love and the struggle with love.' Even more applicable to Lawrence's characters is the observation which follows:

> It is urged against Thomas Hardy's characters that they do unreasonable things – quite, quite unreasonable things. They are always going off unexpectedly and doing something that nobody would do. That is quite true, and the charge is amusing. These people of Wessex are always bursting suddenly out of bud and taking a wild flight into flower, always shooting suddenly out of a tight convention, a tight, hide-bound cabbage state into something quite madly personal.

The distinction which he goes on to make between 'explosive' characters (the majority of Hardy's, in Lawrence's view) and 'consecutive' ones (of whom Jude is the single example) has more bearing on Lawrence's later fiction than on Hardy's.

Lawrence's *Study* is perhaps the outstanding example in English of criticism which sheds lights on the critic rather than on his subject. But when the critic happens to be a novelist of genius this is hardly to be regretted. Lawrence is factually misleading on a number of topics – he makes Tess a kinswoman of Alec and gives Eustacia Vye Italian ancestry, for example. The factual inaccuracies and the extreme subjectivism melt into insignificance under the emotional heat generated by Lawrence's passionate concern with the issues he raises. But it would be wrong to think of Hardy as just the peg on which Lawrence hangs his own interests. His central importance for Lawrence was twofold. First, Hardy was the great exemplar of the provincial writer of genius who compelled the literary world to listen to him, even though he had to compromise with the conventions of that world in order to do so, just as his characters were in different ways defeated by their society in their efforts to break out of the 'tight, hide-bound cabbage state' and 'come into being'. Secondly, Hardy illustrated both the necessity of a philosophical outlook for the novelist seriously interested in his art, and the dangers of the art becoming only a handmaiden to the philosophy instead of a kind of antagonist or critic of it. As Lawrence himself put it in the *Study*:

> Because a novel is a microcosm, and because man in viewing the universe must view it in the light of a theory, therefore every novel must have the background or the structural skeleton of some theory of being, some metaphysic. *But the metaphysic must always subserve the artistic purpose beyond the artist's conscious aim.* Otherwise the novel becomes a treatise. (My italics.)

Where Hardy had failed, due to compromise or excessive concern for the philosophy at the expense of the truth of his fictions, Lawrence was determined to succeed. It is worth remembering that the *Study of Thomas Hardy* was written at the very time that Lawrence was working on the material of his two greatest novels, *The Rainbow* and *Women in Love*.

Lawrence and Romanticism

One of the dangers of talking about a great writer in relation to a literary tradition is that we are liable to assimilate him too readily into the tradition, smoothing out his individuality into bland membership of a group. We often forget that no important artist 'takes his place' inertly within a tradition, like a man moving into furnished lodgings. Rather, he radically reshapes it by his distinctive contribution. Indeed, the effort to get at the distinctive and original quality of a writer ought to be the only *critical* reason for trying to relate him to a tradition at all.

In the case of Lawrence, his relationship to Romanticism is at once superficially obvious and yet fundamentally elusive, or at any rate unstable. Among other things, the attempt to relate the two reminds us of the many and various things signified by the term 'Romanticism' even if we restrict it, as I shall do here, to its context in English literature. We may notice how some well known utterances by the English Romantics seem to encapsulate certain aspects of Lawrence's achievement and outlook. I am thinking of such axioms as Blake's 'without contraries is no progression', Wordsworth's 'wise passiveness', Keats' sense of 'the holiness of the heart's affections' and Coleridge's view of the primary imagination as 'essentially *vital*, even as all objects (*as* objects) are essentially fixed and dead'. In their rough and ready way all these and similar comments point towards important elements in Lawrence, but separately and collectively they are quite inadequate to do more than suggest the area of thought and imagination within which Lawrence's creative genius achieved its flowering. The nature of that achievement can properly be indicated only in the terms Lawrence himself carved out, and some account of it will be attempted in the central section of this study.

One of the fundamental Romantic insights which Lawrence made thoroughly his own was the double vision of a living universe and of man's true fulfilment being dependent on being *rooted* in it. It was a vision shaped in fierce reaction to the mechanistic cause-and-effect rigidity of the new science, what Blake called 'the single vision and Newton's sleep'. Bertrand Russell, who would have been proud to acknowledge intellectual kinship with Newtonian science, once said of Lawrence (before he decided that Lawrence was a dangerous precursor of Fascism) that he was 'just like Shelley – just as fine, but with a similar impatience of fact'. There is a sense in which this is true, but it is not the sense which goes on to infer that Lawrence was some kind of lunatic repeatedly banging his solar plexus and denying what was plainly so. Lawrence was impatient of facts in the same sense that Coleridge was when he said that all objects *as* objects are essentially fixed and dead. He did not deny, any more than Coleridge did, the practical utility of certain ways of thinking about the world – what may loosely be called the technological attitude, the attitude which regards the material world as 'out there', and unrelated to human beings except as an object of manipulation and control. Nor did he deny the necessity of regarding human beings themselves in analogous ways – as average units with certain quantifiable needs– for specific administrative and political purposes, though he insisted that these be kept to the barest minimum. But he denied vehemently and incessantly that these ways of regarding man and the world were either absolute truths by which other kinds of truth were to be judged and found wanting or that any sensible and lasting conception of human fulfilment could be framed in their terms alone. Confronted as we are fifty years after his death by a technological impasse and a growing dubiety about either the possibility or the desirability of continued growth in productivity as the panacea for all ills, and with the Third World poised to make the catastrophic errors with which the West is still struggling, it would be a bold spirit who asserted that Lawrence was wrong. He believed, and he was thoroughly in the Romantic tradition in believing, that man's relation to the world he lived in and to his fellow human beings were inseparable questions and the most important questions that could be asked; that the answer to the first which proposed an 'objective' universe and a 'subjective' knower was, in essential matters, a calamitous mis-construction of the situation; and that the answer to the second lay in a truer understanding of the first, which would yield insights into a more human interconnection between people than any that modern society or current political ideology offered.

The metaphor through which Lawrence most persistently expressed this vision in poetry, fiction and discursive prose was also central to the Romantic imagination. It is the metaphor of the Tree of Life. It takes many forms in Lawrence, as it does in the Romantics, though no single Romantic poet invests it with the richness that he did. Sometimes the tree is human life rooted in the cosmos, sometimes the cosmos itself is the tree, in which the human species, or the individual is bud, leaf or flower. A characteristically distinctive variant of the metaphor occurs in the credo Lawrence wrote into his essay on Benjamin Franklin:

That I am I.
That my soul is a dark forest.
That my known self will never be more than a little clearing in the forest.
That gods, strange gods, come forth from the forest into the clearing of my known self, and then go back.
That I must have the courage to let them come and go.
That I will never let mankind put anything over me, but that I will always try to recognize and submit to the gods in me and the gods in other men and women.

Studies in Classic American Literature.

This was first written at the beginning of the war. In a poem written towards the end of his life, the tree stands as an image of the possibility of fulfilment for the individual:

I don't want to be poor, it means I am pinched.
But neither do I want to be rich.
When I look at this pine-tree near the sea,
that grows out of rock and plumes forth, plumes forth,
I see it has a natural abundance.

With its roots it has a grand grip on its daily bread,
and its plumes look like green cups held up to sun and air
and full of wine.
I want to be like that, to have a natural abundance
and plume forth, and be splendid.

'Poverty'.

Here the focus of the image is narrowed to the single life; in an essay of the same period it takes on a far wider resonance:

For the truth is, we are perishing for lack of fulfilment of our greater needs, we are cut off from the great sources of our inward nourishment and renewal, sources which flow eternally in the universe.

Vitally, the human race is dying. It is like a great uprooted tree, with its roots in the air. We must plant ourselves again in the universe.

'A Propos of *Lady Chatterley's Lover*'.

In another late essay, the essentially *un*selfish nature of Lawrentian fulfilment is clear, when the individual's moral duty to look beyond his own limited time perspective finds expression once again in the central Romantic metaphor:

> Because I know the tree will ultimately die, shall I therefore refrain from planting seed? Bah! it would be conceited cowardice on my part. I love the little sprout and the weak little seedling. I love the thin sapling, and the first fruit, and the falling of the first fruit. I love the great tree in its splendour. And I am glad that at last, at the very last, the great tree will grow hollow, and fall on its side with a crash, and the little ants will run through it, and it will disappear like a ghost back into the humus.
>
> 'On Human Destiny'.

(It is characteristic of Lawrence that even his most portentous writing is veined with a fine literalism of fact – little ants are liable to run through even his most gigantic metaphors.) It is the central idea of rootedness, of man's relationship to the rest of creation that takes the main weight in Lawrence's handling of the metaphor. Opposed to the image of the tree which stands for the living universe, man's true connection with it and through it with his fellow men is the mechanical connection of men to each other through money and machines and to mechanical and unliving modes of knowing. The machine is the great Lawrentian symbol of separateness and deadness and its typical motion, that of turning wheels, the very model of meaningless, deadening activity, turned in on itself, with no reference to the rest of the universe:

> Do not think that a machine is without a soul.
> Every wheel on its hub has a soul, evil,
> it is part of the evil world-soul, spinning.

'The Evil World-Soul'.

And just as man's relation to the machine can never be other than dead and soulless, so exclusively mental knowledge of the world and of life can only exile man from his true inheritance. Lawrence sometimes wrote as if mental consciousness were altogether expendable and 'blood consciousness' or intuitive apprehension all that human beings needed. But at the heart of his writing in criticism, exposition, poetry and fiction is the clear conviction that it is the *supremacy* of mental and quantitative knowledge which needs to be dethroned, with its consequent excessive sway in inappropriate areas of life and its claim to exclusiveness. In its plainest form, we find this central doctrine in a few lines from a poem significantly entitled 'Climb Down, O Lordly Mind – ':

> A man is many things, he is not only a mind.
> But in his consciousness, he is two-fold at least:
> he is cerebral, intellectual, mental, spiritual,
> but also he is instinctive, intuitive, and in touch.
>
> The mind, that needs to know all things
> must needs at last come to know its own limits,
> even its own nullity, beyond a certain point.

What was most urgently needed therefore, in Lawrence's view was a 'climbing down' on the part of the mental consciousness and the recognition of man's relation to a living cosmos – 'life consists not in facts, but a flow'.

The idea of the noble savage and the associated myth of an ideal primitive society which later ones may profitably try to emulate both go back beyond Romanticism as a literary-artistic movement, at least as far back as the early days of European colonization. But both received new impetus and memorable formulations from the Romantics in their reaction against the constrictive forms of their own society. At a certain stage of his development Lawrence was drawn to both ideas, and his own efforts to found an ideal Rananim may be regarded as evidence of this. But he had decisively rejected both notions by the time he came to write his most important works, *The Rainbow* and *Women in Love*. Both novels are informed by the conviction that the way ahead lies *through* the chaos of modern life and society rather than in turning one's back on it, though for Lawrence the man the temptation towards the latter was sometimes almost overwhelming. He wrote his own epitaph on his Utopian endeavours in his essay on Crevecoeur in *Studies in Classic American Literature* (significantly with a reference to a similar project by Coleridge):

> A new world, a world of the Noble Savage and Pristine Nature and Paradisal Simplicity and all that gorgeousness that flows out of the unsullied fount of the ink-bottle. Lucky Coleridge who got no further than Bristol, some of us have gone all the way.

Both the noble savage and the ideal primitive society were rejected by Lawrence not because they were undesirable but for the more fundamental reason that they were unattainable because self-contradictory. What had attracted Lawrence to the idea of the noble savage was not what some Romantic writers had seen in the figure – one whose moral nature had not been corrupted by civilization, who displayed the virtues of courage, honour, loyalty and so forth considered native to man; it was rather the notion of primitive man as being closer to the primal sources of life, undistracted by self-consciousness and merely intellectual awareness. In its extreme form, the myth becomes in Lawrence an idealization of pure animal existence, literally regarding the unselfconscious *being* of animals (and even plants) as a possible human ideal. In one of his verse fragments Lawrence talks about the gaiety of a bird as it flips its tail, getting its balance on a bough and wistfully asks: 'Why can't people be gay like that?' But in another poem, contrasting man and bat, he shows his awareness that 'the human soul is fated to wide-eyed responsibility/In life'. Completely unselfconscious being is not possible as a permanent human condition. It is the combination of being and knowledge-of-being or consciousness that defines the human animal, leading both to the glories and the anxieties of being human:

> No, no, let man be as primitive as primitive can be, he still has a mind ... Let us dismiss the innocent child of nature. He does not exist, never did, never will, and never could. No matter at what level man may be, he still has a mind, he also has passions. And the mind and the passions between them beget the scorpion brood of ideas. Or, if you like, call it the angelic hosts of the ideal.

'On Human Destiny'.

Even the emotions cannot 'run free, without the dead hand of the ideal mind upon them':

> It is impossible. Because once man ate the apple and became endowed with mind, or mental consciousness, the human emotions are like a wedded wife; lacking a husband, she is only a partial thing. The emotions cannot be "free".

The first step towards freeing the self from the shackles of mental consciousness is, paradoxically, the *intellectual* awareness of the necessity to do so – 'the mind must ... at last come to know its own limits'. Beyond this, Lawrence envisaged a state of receptivity which has something in common with the Wordsworthian 'wise passiveness', though characteristically the emphasis in Lawrence is on a more positive preparedness, an awakening of non-mental centres of consciousness (about which something will be said in the discussion of Lawrence and Freudian psychology). 'Not I, but the wind that blows through me', the first line of one of his poems (from which Frieda took the title of her autobiography), speaks of the need for active, full-bodied assent in letting oneself be borne on the wind of time's new direction. The urgent rhythm and excited tone suggest a positive commitment rather than an inert passivity:

Not I, not I, but the wind that blows through me!
A fine wind is blowing the new direction of Time.
If only I let it bear me, carry me, if only it carry me!
If only I am sensitive, subtle, oh, delicate, a winged gift!

'Song of a Man who has Come Through'.

The sense of human life as part of a more inclusive organic whole and the consequent need for an attitude of reverent awareness point towards paradox and contrariety, both as a *means* of reaching a truer apprehension of the world about us and within us and also as part of the *content* of that apprehension. The two are connected, of course. True awareness, in the Lawrentian view, not come from an analytical point-by-point chain of reasoning, but rather from the collision of opposed apprehensions – 'without contraries is no progression'. Where Lawrence the imaginative writer is concerned, the most important implication of this view and one that will be discussed later both in relation to Lawrence's criticism and his practice as a novelist, is that there is, or should be, a problematic relationship between the novelist's message and the fiction in which that message is embodied – the final 'message' in other words is the interaction between the medium *and* the message. But paradox is a necessary mode of awareness because it is characteristic of the Lawrentian vision of existence itself. Opposites are not seen as statically apart and in confrontation with each other but as complementarities in dynamic relation to each other. Love and hate, decay and renewal, life and death – all these are the systole and diastole of the total movement, ceaselessly interconnected. In a series of six essays written soon after the outbreak of the First World War (that is, at the time he was working on *The Rainbow* and *Women in Love*), Lawrence used the unifying metaphor of the lion and the unicorn and their struggle for the crown to symbolize this dialectical view of things. Reading through these essays is like blundering through thick fog across uneven and unknown territory, and the reader often bumps painfully into notions whose shape and significance he can only dimly make out. For all that, these essays are among Lawrence's most important non-fictional prose. Again and again, through innumerable images and analogies, he hammers away at the centrality of paradox in our experience of things. And one of the most crucial and wide-ranging of these paradoxes is, as Colin Clarke has pointed out, a basic one in Romantic poetry. As Lawrence applies it to his exploration of sexual experience and feeling in his later novels, it transforms our understanding of Keats' phrase 'the holiness of the heart's affections' by bringing it into violent contact in our minds with lines like Yeats': 'For love has pitched his mansion in/The place of excrement'. It is the paradox of growth rooted in corruption, renewal springing from reduction, sexual health from perversity, exaltation from degeneration. It is through the recognition that the beauty and mystery of God's creation contained not only the evident miracles of bird, sea and sky but also the slimy and monstrous phosphorescence of the writhing sea creatures that Coleridge's Ancient Mariner won through to a perilous grace. ('I'd like to know Coleridge when Charon has rowed me over,' wrote Lawrence in a wartime letter.) Lawrence expresses a similar insight in related imagery in 'The Crown':

> The snake is the spirit of the great corruptive principle, the festering cold of the marsh. This is how he seems, as we look back. We revolt from him, but we share the same life and tide of life as he.

As always, what is true of the great world outside is also, for Lawrence, true of the little world of man. In another important essay of the same period, he relates the image specifically to the individual self:

> There is a natural marsh in my belly, and there the snake is naturally at home. Shall he not crawl into my consciousness? Shall I kill him with sticks the moment he lifts his flattened head on my sight? Shall I kill him or pluck out the eye which sees him? None the less, he will swarm within the marsh.
> Then let the serpent of living corruption take his place among us honourably.
>
> 'Reality of Peace', 1917.

This aspect of Lawrence's relation to Romantic modes of thought and feeling is perhaps the most disturbing element in Lawrence but it is importantly present in his fiction and poetry as well as his quasi-philosophical writings and it should not be ignored.

Like all the great Romantics, Lawrence was passionately concerned about man in society. This concern is most apparent in what he wrote from and including *The Rainbow* onwards, but it is present even in a comparatively early novel like *Sons and Lovers* as we shall see later. In a late essay called 'The State of Funk' he avowedly separated his field of concern from adjacent areas:

> As a novelist, I feel it is the change inside the individual which is my real concern. The great social change interests me and troubles me, but it is not my field. I know a change is coming and I know we must have a more generous, more human system based on the life values and not on the money values. That I know. But what steps to take I don't know. Other men know better.
> My field is to know the feelings inside a man, and to make new feelings conscious.

But this neat division between the exploration of feelings and the understanding of social change is foreign to the tradition from which

Lawrence stems, to his own deepest instincts as a man and to his practice as a writer. If this were not so, if he really had confined himself to some imagined 'inner life' he would probably have been a lesser artist, and he would certainly not have been the target of specifically political accusations, the most frequent of which is that he was a Fascist. It is difficult to discuss the charge of fascism sensibly when the word itself is applied indiscriminately to a wide variety of people and movements, from teachers who believe in a measure of discipline in the classroom to states whose existence depends on secret police and systematic torture. The most one can do is to make a few simple but necessary distinctions and offer some tentative conclusions. Fascism as a political movement had barely got under way before the thirties and Lawrence died in 1930. In essays and letters Lawrence writes with disgust and contempt of the violent behaviour of mobs of Italian Fascists (see, for instance, the Epilogue written in 1924 to *Movements in European History*). In novels such as *Kangaroo* and the *The Plumed Serpent* he explored the problem of political leadership, the relation between the mass and the leader, and the directions of social change. In none of these areas are his views (in so far as they can be teased out of the novels) specifically Fascist in a definable political sense. In particular, the novels test certain authoritarian views; they do not proclaim them. Lawrence's 'religion of the blood' has often been associated with the holocaust into which Hitler hurled Europe. In particular Bertrand Russell asserted that it 'led straight to Auschwitz'. It seems to me that the Lawrentian effort to live from non-mental centres of consciousness is literally poles apart from the willed doctrine of racial supremacy leading to systematic extermination practised by the Nazis. Lawrence spoke of the white and dark races, but not in terms which could justify the subjugation of one by the other (though it must be admitted that by and large he took the British Empire for granted as A Good Thing). The state, to Lawrence, could never be a reasonable object of a free man's worship. Finally, Lawrence affirmed his faith in an aristocracy, but a natural, not a social one; he specifically wrote more than once that the old hereditary aristocracy was washed out. His views on education were the opposite of Fascist ideas of regimentation and indoctrination.

We can do no more here than note that the anti-democratic strain in some of the greatest twentieth-century writers – Eliot, Yeats, Pound, Lawrence – is too persistent to be mere coincidence. In Lawrence's case the bitter contempt for many aspects of modern living has often been confused with hatred of life itself, not always without reason. Lawrence does occasionally unite with a strain in Fascist thinking, but his fierce opposition to the money-madness of capitalist society and its dehumanizing cash-deformed human relationships is at the very heart of his social thought. His impassioned attacks on the material greed, hypocrisy and sheer inhumanity of modern society are founded not on a beehive model of a totalitarian society but on a notion of human freedom which can *only* be found in relatedness. 'Thank God I am not free, any more than a rooted tree is free,' expresses the Lawrentian ideal of freedom. The final stress must fall on the essentially religious view which Lawrence took of man's relationship with the cosmos. It was because the forms of modern social and economic organization violated this relationship that he hated them and wanted them changed. His practical programmes for change, such as they were, may not have been either impressive or particularly practical (though many of his educational ideas are now widely accepted and successfully practised). The first necessity, in Lawrence's own apocalyptic language, was to realize the need for 'the one glorious activity of man: the getting himself into a new relationship with a new heaven and a new earth'.

Lawrence's quarrel with Freud

As explained earlier, Lawrence's first contact with Freudian ideas probably came when he met Frieda in 1912. Several years before this Frieda had had an affair with Otto Gross, a disciple of Freud, and through him she obtained some first-hand if unsystematic knowledge of the ideas and attitudes of the Freudian circle in Vienna. The influence of Freudian ideas on *Sons and Lovers*, especially in the handling of the mother–son relationship, may be attributed to Frieda's collaboration (though that is too emphatic a word) on the later stages of that novel. But Lawrence's sustained interest in Freudian psychology came only after the publication of *Sons and Lovers* and the keen interest it aroused among Freudians in England and America. In particular it led to the friendship between Lawrence and Dr David Eder, a colleague of Ernest Jones and the first man to lecture in England on Freud's discoveries.

But Lawrence's relationship to Freudian ideas is not a simple matter of 'explaining' *Sons and Lovers* in terms of the Oedipus complex. Lawrence himself 'hated' the review of his novel on these lines which appeared in the American *Psychoanalytic Review*. Such an account totally distorts the real and important differences which divide the great psychologist from the great creative novelist. These differences go to the very heart of Lawrence's conception of character, morality and social behaviour and shape his educational and political ideas. He himself considered them so important that he tried several times to expound them in a systematic fashion, though Lawrence's idea of a system was more like a river or a tree than a steam engine or the proof of a theorem. His vision was both comprehensive and intensely unique, so that his writings on any one subject or aspect of human experience are constantly flowing into another. His two most sustained pieces of writing on the topic of psychoanalysis and psychology were both written in the early 1920s. They are *Psychoanalysis and the Unconscious* and the longer and later essay *Fantasia of the Unconscious*. Both were written explicitly as polemics against what Lawrence believed to be certain profoundly mistaken ideas in Freudian theory. They are therefore best understood against a general background of Freud's own ideas.

Freud's collected works run into several volumes and contain much discussion of a highly clinical and technical kind, even a short résumé of which would be beyond the scope both of this book and its author. What is attempted in the following paragraphs is a brief statement of certain basic Freudian ideas on which Lawrence's views were radically different. The summary is intended only to set Lawrence's own ideas on these and related topics in as clear a light as possible, not to do full justice to Freudian theory. The reader who wishes to pursue Freud's ideas at first hand may find it helpful to know that my account is based on two important early works, *The Interpretation of Dreams* (1900) and *Three Essays on The Theory of Sexuality* (1905), and two later ones, *Totem and Taboo* (1912) and *Civilization and Its Discontents* (1930).

The ordinary reader probably associates both Freud and Lawrence with certain vague but firmly held notions such as 'Everything is basically to do with sex' and 'It's the unconscious that really governs people's behaviour'. As in most such cases, the ordinary view is partial rather than false. Sexuality and the unconscious play a dominant part in the thinking of both men, but they mean very different things by 'the unconscious', and these differences in turn shape their very different notions of the nature and function of sexuality (and even morality). For Freud, the unconscious is the most important element in a tripartite structure of the psyche, the other two parts of which are the preconscious and the conscious. The unconscious is utterly selfish and utterly ruthless in its blind desire to satisfy the Pleasure Principle. Its desires are mainly sexual and primitive and are such as the conscious moral or aesthetic sensibility of the individual would regard with abhorrence. Even wishes which are rejected by the conscious mind find their way back into the unconscious. It is therefore completely at odds with any cooperative, societal or moral impulses. If the psyche consisted only of the unconscious, civilization would be impossible.

What makes civilization possible is the fact that the Pleasure Principle is subordinated to the demands of the Reality Principle. The need for man's anarchic, self-gratifying desires to be subordinated to external reality, which of course includes the reality of other people, has created through evolutionary adaptation the preconscious part of the psyche which acts as a kind of intermediary between the unconscious and conscious activity. Thus where the unconscious is dangerous and disruptive, programmed to seek its own gratification and heedless of all else, the preconscious adapts the former's impulses according to the demands of reality. Cultural and moral activity (civilization) is a result of this adaptation.

Since the unconscious is both the most primitive and most powerful element of the psyche and seeks nothing but its own satisfaction, its suppression or control becomes a condition of civilization. But suppressed unconscious impulses do not disappear; they are indestructible. The individual must cope with these suppressions by becoming aware of them and so gaining greater control over them, which is the object of Freudian therapy. But the need to suppress or otherwise control the insatiate urges of the subconscious remains the necessary foundation of society. The degree to which these subconscious impulses have been suppressed is an index to the level of a civilization.

Sexual activity is the chief source of the satisfaction of unconscious impulses and begins in infancy with the auto-erotic (suckling) phase. It then passes through the anal-sadistic and into the phallic phase. It is in this last phase that the child experiences the Oedipal relationship when his experiences of the mother crystallize into desire for her and consequent hatred of the father as rival. But the demands of social reality inhibit the expression of these desires which are 'latent' until puberty, when the individual adapts himself to adult sexual needs, repressing and internalizing his infantile sexual impulses. The mother as focus of sexual desire returns in this later phase of adult sexual consciousness. Liberation from the mother and reconciliation with the father becomes the major task of adult life, a task in which our ideas of guilt, responsibility, conscience and so forth are awakened and developed. Those who fail to come to terms with the need to abandon the wish-fulfilling desire for the mother and make their peace with the reality of the father suffer a regression to an earlier stage of development. The neuroses which the individual suffers are at once the discontents of civilization and the condition of its development. Neurosis and civilization are two sides of the same coin.

Even in this drastically simplified summary, one can see that Freud's is essentially a tragic view of life, with man for ever crucified between reality and desire. It is a view based on his clinical experience and on a profound regard for Darwinian evolutionary ideas. Lawrence's views on the psyche, consciousness and the unconscious and related subjects were the product of sustained reflection on his own individual case, brought to white heat by his experiences in wartime England and tempered by battling his way through to new notions about human nature and morality in his two great novels, *The Rainbow* and *Women in Love*. In his foreword to *Fantasia of the Unconscious* he makes some observations on his expository writings which are widely quoted and often misused: 'This pseudo-philosophy of mine' he writes,

> – 'pollyanalytics', as one of my respected critics might say – is deduced from the novels and poems, not the reverse. The novels and poems come unwatched out of one's pen.

The quotation often stops here and is used as an implicit excuse for not paying any attention to the 'pollyanalytics' except in a condescending and dismissive way. But Lawrence goes on to say:

> And then the absolute need which one has for some sort of satisfactory mental attitude towards oneself and things in general makes one try to abstract some definite conclusions from one's experiences as a writer and as a man. The novels and poems are pure passionate experience. These 'pollyanalytics' are inferences made afterwards, from the experience.

While the novels offer a richer and more complex experience than mere 'dramatization' of metaphysical and psycho-philosophical ideas, the 'absolute need' from which Lawrence wrote was deep and imperious and it produced writing which is worthy of all the alert and sympathetic attention we can give it. To put it in the lowest terms, Lawrence's two 'pollyanalytic' essays are certainly more interesting in themselves and more important to an understanding of his fiction than, say, Yeats' *A Vision* either intrinsically or as a commentary on his poetry.

The principal disagreement which Lawrence had with Freudian theory centres on the nature of the unconscious. For Lawrence, it was at once a much vaster and a much more positive element than it was for Freud. In a brilliantly evocative sentence in *Psychoanalysis and the Unconscious* he writes that 'The Freudian unconscious is the cellar in which the mind keeps its own bastard spawn', while 'The true unconscious is the well-head, the fountain of real motivity.' Lawrence found support for his critique in the views of the American psychologist Trigant Burrow whose book *The Social Basis of Consciousness* (which Lawrence reviewed) argued that the Freudian unconscious was merely the representation of *conscious* sexual life as it exists in a state of repression. Burrow also lent support to another important Lawrentian idea, namely that it was not sex itself that was the original sin, but mental consciousness of sex. It was repressed *ideas* of sex that the Freudian unconscious contained and it was for this reason that Lawrence denied its claim to be 'the pristine unconscious in man'. It was essentially backward looking, always cluttered and clogged up with the debris and detritus of infantile sexuality. For Lawrence, on the contrary, the unconscious was nothing less than the source of life, individuality and above all of the principle of *new* creativity:

What then is the true unconscious? It is not a shadow cast from the mind. It is the spontaneous life motive in every organism. Where does it begin? It begins where life begins.

Acknowledging that such vague language is not very helpful, Lawrence goes on to locate the unconscious as a precise genetic–biological principle, as he later locates non-mental centres of consciousness in various parts of the human anatomy:

Where the individual begins, life begins. The two are inseparable, life and individuality. And also, where the individual begins, the unconscious, which is the specific life-motive, also begins. We are trying to trace the unconscious to its source. And we find that this source in all the higher organisms, is the first ovule cell from which an individual organism arises. At the moment of conception, when a procreative male nucleus fuses with the nucleus of the female germ, at that moment does a new unit of life, of consciousness arise in the universe. Is it not obvious? The unconscious has no other source than this, this first fused nucleus of the ovule.

Psychoanalysis and the Unconscious.

This idea of the unconscious as the principle of individuality and potentiality for the genuinely new in life is crucial to Lawrence's thinking. It explains among other things the radical difference between his account of the incest taboo and Freud's. He denies categorically Freud's theory that the incest taboo derives from some primal crime of patricide and the subsequent need of the sons to live in peace together, all this myth-history being re-enacted in the individual psyche as the Oedipus complex. Far from being a stage of the normal parent child relationship, sexuality enters that relationship *only* through the interference of the mind in the form of an idealization of the mother figure prolonged beyond its normal period. A man who does this finds it impossible to achieve true fulfilment in marriage and 'the emotional, and even passional regard' which is greater for the mother than for the wife forces a terrible choice between incest, insanity and death. The important point is that the incest motive appears *not* as part of the normal development of sex but as a result of idealizing the parental relationship or through premature stimulation of the sexual urge, both examples of mental interference. Lawrence strongly denied that sexuality in a strict sense existed before puberty, and this is a perfectly tenable view insofar as most of Freud's evidence for infantile sexuality seems to be evidence only in a retrospective sense, that is, from the point of view of adult sexuality as a basic, indeed *the* basic, impulse developed. As Lawrence put it:

Sex – that is to say, maleness and femaleness – is present from the moment of birth, and in every act or deed of every child. But sex in the real sense of dynamic sexual relationship, this does not exist in a child, and cannot exist until puberty or after.

Fantasia of the Unconscious.

It is because he placed so high a value on the adult sexual relationship as a sign of a mature, responsible and moral experience that Lawrence denied the existence of infantile sexuality except as an incidental and unimportant aberration.

The idea of the unconscious as the source of genuine individuality and newness meant that the individual was never merely the product of whatever was contributed by his parents. The emphasis is always on individuality as the 'only one supreme quality' with an intrinsic capacity for going beyond itself. It is the primal life force, never found in the abstract but always realized concretely. The unconscious, as life itself, is prior to cause and effect and prior to any form of mental consciousness (which, as has been noted, includes Lawrence's conception of the Freudian unconscious). Here we have the clue to his hostility towards the psychoanalytic method. As far back as 1916 he had told the English Freudian Barbara Low, 'The longer I live, the less I like psychoanalysis.' Even earlier, when Frieda first introduced him to Freud's ideas in 1912, Lawrence had felt that his (Freud's) notions of sex were too limited and mechanistic and that 'the root was deeper'. The root, according to Lawrence, was pre-mental unconscious life. Psychoanalysis as he saw it was a means of imposing mental consciousness on this active, unique life-principle, of attempting to bind it in the shackles of cause and effect. It was also an insidious erosion of the individual's moral responsibility under the guise of therapy, since in the Freudian view repression of unconscious desires lay at the root of moral behaviour.

Thus Lawrence's objections to Freudian psychology and analysis were in the wide sense religious, as he himself realized. He denied the validity of mechanistic procedures in psychoanalytic explanation on the basis of an intuitive conviction, tested in his own experience, of the uniqueness and individuality of living organisms, human or otherwise. And 'mechanistic' in this context comes to the same thing as 'ideal', meaning derived from fixed mental concepts. 'It is obvious that the ideal becomes a mechanical principle if it be applied to the affective soul as a fixed motive,' he writes. And he was not afraid to use the vocabulary of religion in arguing his case:

This causeless created nature of the individual being is the same as the old mystery of the divine nature of the soul. Religion was right and science is wrong. Every individual creature has a soul, a specific individual nature the origin of which cannot be found in any cause-and-effect process whatsoever. Cause-and-effect will not explain even the individuality of a single dandelion. There is no assignable cause, and no logical reason, for individuality. On the contrary, it appears in defiance of all scientific law, in defiance even of reason.

Psychoanalysis and the Unconscious.

Lawrence is here not, of course, denying that causal explanations can be given of the *existence* of dandelions. What he is asserting as a primary article of faith is that their *individuality*, that which makes the individual dandelion itself and no other is beyond the reach of cause and effect. And this 'soul', *newly* created in each individual, is yet subject to time and not immortal, for it can only exist in the individual life, never as an abstract entity or as some homogeneous, unrealized life force.

The problem for human beings is *not* to become consciously aware of their unconscious impulses, for that is merely to force them into a cause and effect straitjacket and to distort their nature and their essentially beneficent power. As Aldous Huxley remarked, while many thinkers have drawn attention to the presence of dark forces in the mind, Lawrence was one of the few who approved of the area of darkness and wished to extend it (though this last phrase is misleading). The real difficulty is to live from the unconscious centres which, as will appear shortly, are the true source not only of individuality but of *relatedness*, between man and man, man and woman, man and the cosmos. The knowledge we should have of the unconscious is 'always a matter of whole experience, what St Paul calls knowing in full, and never a matter of mental conception merely'. This emphasis on the wholeness of experience was also characteristic of the Gestalt school of psychology which was active at the time Lawrence wrote but of which he does not seem to have been aware.

Lawrence's account of the workings of the unconscious, or rather of the non-mental centres of consciousness and their interrelations is probably that part of his psycho–physiological theory which many Western readers will find least sympathetic, though perhaps less so now than in his own lifetime. He begins by asserting that though in its totality the unconscious transcends all laws of cause and effect 'in its processes of self-realization' it follows such laws. Rejecting the vocabulary of science as totally unsuited for his purpose because it was tainted with 'ideal' notions repugnant to him, he was nevertheless convinced of the reality of non-mental consciousness as part of individual experience and therefore necessarily related to the life of the body. So he proposed a scheme of different centres which borrowed some of the terminology of certain Eastern philosophical systems, especially as these had been adapted by the Theosophists in England and America. There were, in the Lawrentian scheme, four such centres, two upper and two lower, two at the front and two at the back. The upper centres, located in the cardiac plexus and the thoracic ganglion, were the sources of intellectual and spiritual activity. While they lie at the root of disinterested enquiry and activity, when they are given a dominant place at the expense of other modes of awareness, as they have been in our culture, they cut the individual off from the deeper sources of his being. The other two centres are located in the lower body, that in the solar plexus making the individual aware of himself as the centre of all things (*not* however, as an 'idea'), and the one in the lumbar ganglion stimulating his sense of uniqueness within the scheme of things.

Whatever we may think of Lawrence's schematization of the psyche, two points are worth making about it. First, that relying almost entirely on intuition and introspection, Lawrence arrived at a schema which had remarkable similarities to ancient non-European ideas about man and his relation to the universe. His reading was always secondary, being determined both in selection and interpretation by certain intuitive ideas. As E. T. (Jessie Chambers) says in her memoir, 'he seemed to regard all philosophical reading from the angle of his own personal need'. Secondly, his scheme allowed Lawrence to account for experience in ways which mechanistic explanations of human behaviour (his principal and most prestigious target at the time) did not. It offered him an interpretation of experience that was at once religious and materialist; located in the body but in touch with the cosmos. For the unconscious, because it is 'never in any sense selfish' (unlike the Freudian unconscious), formed the only basis of a genuine morality. His own schematization might have brought Lawrence perilously near the mechanistic approach he detested so much. But the idea of different centres of consciousness, and their continual interconnections allowed Lawrence the novelist to explore areas of experience which he made peculiarly his own, such as the ebb and flow of emotions and especially the rhythm of love and hate. Where the Freudian view of the psyche saw man as perpetually self-divided, Lawrence saw the possibility of the breach being healed. But Lawrence's too is a potentially tragic vision in that modern society has gone so far astray that the return to a new relatedness presupposes a conscious effort to live from unconscious centres (or at least a conscious recognition of the need to do so), a task continually menaced by artificiality and falseness of feeling. Lawrence was himself uncertain as to how it could be done and in *Fantasia of the Unconscious* talks of a society divided into the small minority of those able to translate unconscious impulses into action and the large mass of people who share these impulses but only in an inarticulate mythical manner:

For the mass of the people knowledge must be symbolical, mythical, dynamic. This means you must have a higher, responsible, conscious class: and then in varying degrees the lower classes, varying in their degree of consciousness.

We seem to be back once more with the domination of society by a more highly conscious class, which was Lawrence's original ground for condemning modern society, modern education and modern civilization as a whole. It is possible that this 'higher, responsible' consciousness is a non-mental one, alert to all modes of awareness, but if so it is difficult to see how it differs from the 'symbolic, mythical, dynamic' knowledge of the masses. Such inconsistencies weaken novels like *Kangaroo* and *The Plumed Serpent* but they do not seriously affect the depth, seriousness and cogency of Lawrence's criticism of modern life.

Lawrence today

Lawrence has been dead for more than fifty years but he shows no signs of lying down. If anything he is more alive today than at any other time in the twentieth century. His novels and short stories continue to be reprinted in enormous quantities and to be translated all over the world. On film, television and radio his fictions have shown their power to hold vast audiences enthralled, and his plays have proved absorbing in performance. His expository writings, until recently apologized for and embarrassedly passed over even by admirers of Lawrence the artist, are being read with a new respect. Professional educators such as G. H. Bantock and William Walsh have paid tribute to his pioneering educational ideas and psychologists such as Norman O. Brown and R. D. Laing have been impressed by his thinking in their fields of professional concern. More and more people in all walks of life are coming to realize that the man whose sense of vital knowledge as opposed to dead facts led him to write: 'The atom? Why, the moment you discover the atom it will explode under your nose', however misguided he may have been, he was not a raving maniac with what T. S. Eliot magisterially called 'an incapacity for what we ordinarily call thinking'. That he had no such incapacity is evident in virtually all his writing. What is equally evident is that he refused to accept 'what we ordinarily call thinking' as the only or even the most important mode of access we have to real understanding and fulfilment. He believed, for instance (for reasons we shall examine later), that the novelist was 'superior to the poet, the philosopher and the saint'. He may have been wrong, but it is important to understand as clearly as he did just what he was trying to say.

Though he had his roots firmly in the Midlands and continued to derive inspiration from the memories of his formative years there, during the more or less continuous exile which was his life, Lawrence is no more a provincial or regional writer than Hardy; indeed much less so, since all Hardy's novels are set in and around his native Wessex. Lawrence founded no school of 'Nottingham writers', though traces of the early Lawrence may be found in Alan Sillitoe's *Saturday Night and Sunday Morning* and one or two of his better short stories and more impressively in such novels as Philip Callow's *Pledge for the Earth* and David Storey's *Radcliffe*. His poetry, long neglected or condescended to in spite of early praise from poet-critics such as Ezra Pound and Conrad Aiken, is at last, in the tired but useful phrase, beginning to get the recognition it deserves and has plainly left its mark on poets such as Ted Hughes and Seamus Heaney. But Lawrence was too original a writer to found a school. He liberated a vast area of human experience for English fiction and every subsequent writer's treatment of sexual relations has been influenced by Lawrence's example, not necessarily for the better. His technical discoveries, though profoundly original, were intimately related to his individual vision. He once declared 'Art for my sake' to be his motto. Technique in Lawrence is not a set of detachable literary devices available for general imitation. Those who try to imitate him usually sound false or foolish or both. Paradoxical as it may sound, the impact of Lawrence's fiction and ideas is difficult to track down precisely because it has been so great over so vast a range. He is one of the few twentieth century figures who have altered the quality of our life and thought even if we are unaware of it and even if we have never read a line he wrote. Once we do read him, there is no mistaking the sound of his voice.

Part Two
Critical Survey

the father to die conveniently early in the narrative. Like many first novels, this one contains more plot material than the author either needs or is interested in, as well as many of the themes of his later work. These include the implications of a 'good marriage' especially for a woman, the nature and possibilities of emotional attachment between men and the obstacles to spontaneous living presented by modern society. *The White Peacock* is autobiographical in the sense that the characters and setting are drawn from Lawrence's personal experience of Haggs Farm and Eastwood, especially of the youthful circle known as the Pagans. But there is a deeper sense in which the novel is not autobiographical at all. It touches on but does not face squarely those disturbing pressures and divisions of family life which shaped both the writer and the man. These could not be exorcised until the relationship with Jessie Chambers had crawled to its slow extinction and, even more important, until the fierce grasp of mother love had loosened its hold in death. These two events, together with his encounter with 'the woman of a lifetime' made it possible for Lawrence to write his truly and honestly autobiographical novel, *Sons and Lovers*.

4 *Sons and Lovers*

Sons and Lovers is too well known to need detailed discussion. But because I have approached the book from the standpoint of Lawrence's personal biography, it is especially necessary to stress at the outset that what Lawrence wrote is a remarkable and fascinating work of fiction which resists all attempts (and there have been several) to shrink it down so that it is no more than a record of its author's psychological problems. One could say that the novel begins with the author's problems but does not end with them. It opens out into the reader's world, illuminating and enhancing it by the depth of its insight and the steady honesty of its vision. 'One sheds one's sicknesses in books,' Lawrence once wrote, and did himself less than justice by the implication of an inert casting off of psychological disturbances into fiction. What we find in *Sons and Lovers*, if we read it without too many preconceptions, is not the passive expression of emotional entanglements as so many involuntary and inescapable symptoms, but the decisive mastery of them into a shaped and shapely work of fiction.

Life into art: the truth of fiction

The shaping of the raw material of life into the form of fiction is what particularly needs stressing. Jessie Chambers, the real life Miriam who wrote her own version of the early relationship between Lawrence and herself, bitterly criticized him for distorting the truth of that relationship under the insidious emotional domination of his mother. In the light of the available evidence, which is quite considerable, it is more than likely that Jessie Chambers was right, though she may have exaggerated the exclusiveness of Lawrence's interest in her. The author of *Sons and Lovers* almost certainly altered, consciously or otherwise, the facts as well as the feelings that existed between his youthful self and Jessie. But the only conclusion that legitimately follows from this, as far as the reader is concerned, is that *Sons and Lovers* should not be considered a true and faithful record of the love affair between two actual human beings in a particular part of the English Midlands in the early years of this century. But nobody is likely to consider it in this way unless already led astray by psycho-analytical or other prejudices. The young girl in the novel is not, after all, called Jessie Chambers but Miriam Leivers, nor is the novel's hero D. H. Lawrence; his name is Paul Morel.

This is not simply a trivial quibble about names. In the case of

Cyril Beardsall in *The White Peacock* one could argue that there is hardly any distance between the character and what we know of the author at the time, though this might be used as an argument for not knowing too much about the author before we read a novel. The situation is complicated by the fact that the character is the narrator as well. But in *Sons and Lovers* Paul Morel is one character among many. Admittedly he is the central character and in an important sense the other characters exist for him (as Lady Macbeth, Banquo and the Witches exist 'for' Macbeth), since it is his emotional, intellectual, social and above all psychic development that the novel portrays. But this does not in any way imply that his is the authoritative voice in the novel and that there is no appeal in the fiction from his judgment on others and evaluations of his own experience. Paul Morel is subject to authorial criticism, both in the form of explicit comment and ironic presentation, far more often than is generally allowed. With a little exaggeration we could say that the most important thing to remember when reading *Sons and Lovers* is that Paul Morel did not write it and *could not* have written all of it. There are reaches of insight and understanding within the novel which are quite clearly beyond the central character. It is useful to remember that the author is looking back in his mid-twenties on his early teenage self. And he is looking back from the vantage point of a strong and fulfilling relationship (with Frieda) on one that was partial, frustrated and doomed to failure.

Son and lover : the unmaking of a hero

Sons and Lovers does not simply present us with a hero who has chosen his mother's side and rejected his father's. Instead it shows us with great subtlety the process by which this choice is gradually made and finally confirmed. Not only certain crucial incidents but the structure of the novel as a whole is designed to show the reader how Paul Morel comes to see the world as he does. By uncovering the sources of Paul's partial vision, the author enables us not to identify it with that of the novel in itself. This is one of the chief justifications for the fact that the account of Mrs Morel's possessive love for William is apparently duplicated, though with far greater intensity, in the relationship between her and Paul. The narrative of William's progress and eventual death charts very accurately and in some detail the basis of the emotional involvement between mother and son. In the first instance the son is a substitute husband, a vicarious source of the emotional fulfilment which Mrs Morel cannot find in her marriage. But almost as important is the way in which the son embodies the mother's burning social aspirations, her ideals of respectability, 'getting on' and being looked up to, in all of which her own marriage has so cruelly disappointed her. On both these counts the father is singled out as the enemy and the son's support enlisted in the struggle against him. And since the mining community was an essentially masculine one, shaped by the needs, desires and authority of the men, the struggle against the father inevitably involved in some degree the acceptance by the sons of 'feminine' values – restraint and gentility in speech, sedentary rather than manual work, temperance, domesticity in preference to social camaraderie and so on.

The novel has barely begun before we see the seven-year-old William in the grip of the opposing pulls of father and mother. Morel senior is clearly identified with the festivities of the Wakes – 'Morel, she knew, was sure to make a holiday of it' – while the mother is not – 'Mrs Morel did not like the Wakes'. The little boy's impatience to set off for the fair even before his mother has got his meal ready aligns him with his father's appetite for jollity, but it is his mother's arrival at the Wakes which really crowns his enjoyment – 'He was tipful of excitement now she had come' – and it is for her that he has got the egg-cups as prizes. Furthermore, William is proud to be seen with his mother because 'no other woman looked such a lady as she did'. The consciousness of being a cut above the rest of the community is already present in the lad. Yet his subjection to the mother is not quite complete for he stays on after she leaves and comes home late from the fair, though not quite so late as his father.

Significantly, the decisive trigger-mechanism which finally excludes Morel from his wife's emotional life is an act whereby the father symbolically tries to preserve his son's masculinity against the mother's attempts to soften and sentimentalize it. Morel cuts off little William's hair because 'Yer non want ter make a wench on 'im', and from then on Mrs Morel ceases to yearn for her husband to return to her emotional circle 'Now she ceased to fret for his love: he was an outsider to her.'

Outwardly William's progress in fulfilling his mother's ideals seems to go forward unimpeded. He wins prizes at school, goes from a clerical job in the local Co-op to one at Nottingham and then scales the dizzy heights of a London law office and can send his mother twenty pounds a year. But he is not quite as tractable as his mother could have wished, for he has too much of his father in him. He is big built and has a flashing temper like Morel senior and has the latter's love of dancing and girls. All this is a source of tension between mother and son, coming to a head in the mother's rudeness to the girls his son meets at dances.

Paul on the other hand has been presented to us from even before his birth as linked to his mother's frustrations and desires in a peculiarly intimate way. Whereas the choice of William as a surrogate through whom to live her inner life was a conscious act determined by her husband's neglect and violence at a particular point in their relationship, the bond with Paul appears to go below Mrs Morel's conscious will. When her drunken husband thrusts her out into the moonlit garden and she experiences a strange lapsing out of herself, she still retains her 'consciousness in the child'. When she looks at the newborn baby 'Her love came up hot in spite of everything' including the fact that she had not wanted it. He is a burden to her though she cannot understand why, and her impulsive decision to call him Paul reminds us that Mrs Morel is cast very much in the mould of her father, George Coppard, 'who drew near in sympathy only to one man, the Apostle Paul'. It seems fair to suggest that while Mrs Morel chooses William as an ally because he happened to be the right age at the time she decided to exclude her husband from her life, Paul is 'chosen' by her at a much deeper and more instinctual level. And correspondingly there is less resistance in Paul to the choice, less of his father to counteract the mother's pressure. He is small and frail, girlish and not athletic, artistic and introverted rather than energetic and outgoing like his brother. He is eager to do domestic jobs associated with the mother, such as baking bread, and (despite burning it on one occasion) evidently quite competent at them. And unlike William he is from the beginning 'so conscious of what other people felt, particularly his mother'. It is characteristic of a certain insensitivity to his *mother's* feelings on William's part that he threatens to beat his father because *he* has beaten her, and cannot understand why his mother should be so upset at the idea.

The mother as moulder: failure and success

There is therefore a double movement which determines the structure of the first part of *Sons and Lovers*. The initial impetus for both movements is the mother's disillusionment with and rejection of the father which occurs almost at the very beginning of the novel. As a result of this we see her choose her eldest son as a substitute, but her efforts to mould him exactly to her heart's desire are not entirely successful. By contrast, her younger son is so devotedly and dedicatedly his mother's boy that it almost disturbs Mrs Morel at times. From one point of view we can see William as gradually slipping loose from his mother's stranglehold even though he bears its marks to the end. His moving to London, his insistence on going out with girls his mother disapproves of, his failure to keep up his payments to her are all signs of the recalcitrant element – his father's legacy, we may call it – within him. His death therefore, harrowing as it is for the mother, may yet have forestalled a more bitter defeat for her.

With Paul the victory is hers almost before the battle has begun. From the beginning he offers no resistance to her claims on him and his antipathy to his father is both more passionate and more subtle than William's. There are several ways in which the novel shows up Paul's allegiance to his mother and hostility to his father. The first is by the gradual absorption by Paul of the moral judgments directed by the mother against her husband. Thus in the early episode where Mrs Morel is waiting for Morel senior to return home(Ch. IV), Paul learns to share all his mother's impatience and irritability towards his father. His fearsome private prayer is the direct result of this indoctrination: '"Lord, let my father die," he prayed very often'. (Ch. IV.) Similarly, Paul, like his mother, learns to resent bitterly Morel's prodigality at the public house, while the mother's extravagance over dishes and flowers, smaller though it is in scale, becomes a matter for rejoicing. Paul is also shown entering into a kind of conspiracy with his brother and sister to keep the father from knowing what goes on in the family:

> He was shut out from all family affairs. No one told him anything. The children, alone with their mother, told her all about the day's happenings, everything. Nothing had really taken place in them until it was told to their mother. But as soon as the father came in everything stopped. (Ch. IV)

Though this is offered as a generalization applying to all the family, it is only Paul to whom it is specifically shown as apt, in the incident of the prize he won in the children's paper 'But he would rather have forfeited the prize than have to tell his father'. (Ch. IV.)

Linguistic discrimination and financial independence are two further areas in which Paul is shown enthusiastically taking his mother's side. Morel senior is shown as entirely confined to a dialect which, though the mother found it exotically fascinating in the early days of their courtship, she now despises and cannot understand. (Interestingly, Lawrence often reverts to this dialect for dialogue of especial emotional tenderness, notably in *Lady Chatterley's Lover*.) Furthermore, Morel senior is also virtually inarticulate in his domestic setting except when he is actively engaged in some household task. Paul too has his moments of being tongue-tied, as when he goes to collect his father's wages and at the interview with Mr Jordan. But in his relations with his mother he is jubilantly free with words and his language is the genteel English of Mrs Morel, not the rich coarse dialect of his father. Indeed, there are times when Paul's language takes on the metaphor and rhythms of his mother's. And from speaking a language which shuts out the father it is a short and easy step to expropriating him, at least partially, from his role as breadwinner. Paul's keenest delight in his new job is the opportunity it offers to lay all his wages before his mother, especially as his rival William has defaulted on his early promises of money. All these developments come to a head when Morel senior is injured at work and has to go into hospital, so that Paul is literally the man about the house, a point which he eagerly seizes on – '"I'm the man in the house now", he used to say to his mother with joy.' (Ch. V.)

Thus partly by contrast with William's progress and partly in its own right the gradual emotional crippling of Paul by his mother is carefully established in the early stages of the novel. But this is done by the novelist D. H. Lawrence who is able to see, with an intense yet detached sympathy – such as many of us have for our younger selves – the predicament of Paul Morel. If we fail to see this we are denying ourselves a perspective on the hero's future development which *Sons and Lovers* quite plainly offers us.

Women in a man's world

There are three principal female characters in *Sons and Lovers* (four if we include Miriam's mother). The real life counterpart of one of them (Miriam) actually had a hand in the making of the novel and may even have written some passages in it. Another, Lawrence's mother, is quite clearly not only the presiding influence but at certain points almost the final cause, not only the person the novel is about but the one it is written for. The third, the real life counterpart of Clara Dawes (or one of them – Frieda also contributed something to Clara), is a shadowier figure who may have initiated Lawrence into sexual intercourse. As the pattern of the novel's earlier part is that of Paul's progressive succumbing to his mother's power, so the pattern of the later and longer sections is that of Paul's all but futile attempt to break free of the mother and find a fulfilling relationship with another woman. Part of the fascination and distinction of the novel lies in the fact that although it is principally concerned with Paul's desperate voyage out, it also depicts the women who surround him as independent centres of existence with desires and aspirations of their own which are quickened into life by Paul but neither dominated nor fulfilled by him. The association with Frieda doubtless gave Lawrence the freedom and detachment from his past necessary for this kind of presentation.

Paul's crucial emotional relationship is of course with his mother. Of the other two women with whom he becomes involved, Miriam enters far more deeply into his life than Clara Dawes. In comparison with the strength and intensity with which the Miriam – Paul relationship is depicted, that between Paul and Clara is meagre and superficial and has a good deal of wish fulfilment only just below the surface. Here it would seem that Lawrence the novelist and his hero are at one, for neither seems to be especially interested in the feminism which is evidently an important element in Clara's outlook. Paul talks of Clara to his mother as 'a suffragette and so on' but seems to imply, with no dissenting voice from the author, that her advanced feminist views are merely the result of emotional frustration in her marriage. In fact, while all the women in *Sons and Lovers*, including

Miriam's mother, are presented as frustrated in one way or another, it is only in the case of Mrs Morel that the social and economic roots of this frustration, as opposed to the psychological ones, become a matter of interest for the novelist. If he had taken Clara Dawes and her views more seriously, instead of dismissing them with a kind of amused irony, she might have provided a perspective from which the inadequacies of the other two women might have appeared not purely personal and psychological. Thus Miriam's much talked of 'spirituality' is clearly an inheritance from her mother's deep religious feeling. But that feeling may itself be, what it so often is, in part a kind of unconscious (or perhaps conscious) compensation for a life of ceaseless drudgery in which men make the decisions while women cook, wash and keep house for them. One way to live with such a deadening routine is to sanctify it, to offer it up as one's personal sacrifice to God, which is what Mrs Leivers does. As for Miriam herself, Lawrence comes very close to laying bare the roots of her alleged spirituality and the possessiveness in her which Paul both fears and hankers for. We are told how Miriam's dissatisfaction with the narrow round of her life has been intensified by her reading and education. Her yearning to widen her intellectual horizons and part of her possessiveness towards Paul are aspects of her desperate struggle to escape from the constriction of a woman's life on the farm where her brothers treat her deepest interests and desires with affectionate contempt.

In the early years of the century women had more opportunities for education than for satisfying employment. The result was a growing awareness of the disparity between their own sense of possibility and society's confining hold over them. In the political sphere this led in the years before the First World War to a series of suffragette riots all over Europe and in England to Mrs Pankhurst's Women's Social and Political Union. Through the Eastwood circle which gathered at William Hopkin's house Lawrence would have had first-hand acquaintance with the ideas and ideals of such groups. Clara Dawes is a child of this time and in presenting her as amusingly 'advanced' Lawrence missed an opportunity of adding a social and political dimension to the psychological frustrations of the women which he presents with such extraordinary insight. But it would be pointless to develop this line of criticism further, since blaming an author for not writing a different book is unrewarding. In any case the later Lawrence would certainly have denied the primacy of political and social factors in individual life. What can be usefully pointed out is that a leading theme in much of Lawrence's later fiction is that of the woman in search of a life more creative and fulfilling than that which her milieu prescribes for her. It is the mainspring of many of his short stories and lies at the heart of his two greatest novels, *The Rainbow* and *Women in Love*.

Sons and Lovers *and the English novel*

There are many reasons for regarding *Sons and Lovers* as a pioneering achievement in English fiction. To begin with, as has been pointed out frequently, it is the first great novel of English working class life and the first to be observed from within. There is still nothing in English fiction to match the depth and sympathy with which the everyday life of the Morel household is depicted in the first part of the book. From this point of view, *Sons and Lovers* can be seen as a triumphant culmination of the many nineteenth-century efforts to give a true and full picture of industrial life, among the most impressive of which are George Eliot's *Felix Holt, the Radical*, Mrs Gaskell's *North and South* and parts of Gissing's *Born in Exile* and *Demos*. Lawrence's novel is also an outstanding example of the kind of novel to which the German term *bildungsroman* is sometimes applied, being centrally concerned with the formative years and growth into full awareness of a single character. Where this central figure is an artist, we have a convenient sub-division sometimes called *kunstlerroman* and of this form the two great instances in twentieth-century English fiction are *Sons and Lovers* and Joyce's *Portrait of the Artist as a Young Man*. Though the theme of Paul Morel's artistic development is usually submerged under that of his relationship to his mother, the two are intimately connected; the first surfaces quite clearly at the end of the hero's desperate resolve to turn away from the mother and the drift towards death and set his feet towards a new life in the beckoning city.

But to lay the stress on these aspects of the novel would be to do less than justice to its achievement in opening up new frontiers for fiction. *Sons and Lovers*, as Frank O'Connor pointed out in *The Mirror in the Roadway*, begins like a nineteenth-century realistic novel but ends as a twentieth-century exploratory one. It stands in an oblique relation to the central tradition of the English novel whose main concern is with moral choices, their significance and their consequences. The great English novelists – Fielding, Richardson, George Eliot, Jane Austen, Dickens – are able to show us with compassion and insight how they judge their characters and their actions. Lawrence's fiction came more and more to be concerned not with morality in the ordinary sense but with the psychic ebb and flow within and between characters – 'the flow and recoil of feeling' as he once called it. The nearest anticipation, and it is not really very near at all, is in *Wuthering Heights*. This tracing of a psychic rhythm was, in Lawrence's view, a highly moral inquiry since it was an exploration of the individual's deepest self. But it is not what we ordinarily understand by moral judgments. And over and over again in *Sons and Lovers* we have the feeling that it is *through* the presentation of a given experience that the novelist is finding out for himself what its true meaning is. And as often as not there is a residue of mystery, a sense of unexplained significance pressing in on the experience which the novelist is content to leave hovering about the scene. At its worst this can be merely an irritating mystification, a reaching out after a significance which the novelist is unable to express. But more often what we have is a conviction of the intensity of the felt experience and an apprehension of the mystery which is inherent in it, not of the author's inability to realize it. A passage such as the following from 'Strife in Love' (Ch. VIII) may stand for many throughout the novel:

> And he, coming home from his walks with Miriam, was wild with torture. He walked biting his lips and with clenched fists, going at a great rate. Then, brought up against a stile, he stood for some minutes, and did not move. There was a great hollow of darkness fronting him; and on the black upslopes patches of tiny lights, and in the lowest trough of the night, a flare of the pit. It was all weird and dreadful. Why was he torn so, almost bewildered, and unable to move? Why did his mother sit at home and suffer? He knew she suffered badly. But why should she? And why did he hate Miriam, and feel so cruel towards her, at the thought of his mother. If Miriam caused his mother suffering, then he hated her – and he easily hated her. Why did she make him feel as if he were uncertain of himself, insecure, an indefinite thing, as if he had not sufficient sheathing to prevent the night and the space breaking into him? How he hated her! And then, what a rush of tenderness and humility!

The hollow of darkness, the little lights and the flaring pit become an utterly convincing landscape of the mind without losing any of their objective reality, but they do not explain Paul's emotional turmoil in handy symbols. If we feel we understand his state of mind better than he does himself, that awareness is itself tinged with a sense of tentativeness and uncertainty. *Sons and Lovers* opened out for English fiction a whole new territory of psychic relationships, which required a radical modification of conventional ideas of character, plot and moral significance. It is a territory which was most impressively charted by Lawrence himself in his later fiction.

5 *The Rainbow*

The Rainbow is Lawrence's second longest book, and is in many ways unique among his novels. It originally began as a larger work, *The Sisters*, and included material which was later used in *Women in Love*. Lawrence wrote no less than eight separate versions of the book before he was finally satisfied with it, and even then he had to make certain alterations before the publishers would accept it When it eventually appeared in 1915, in spite of one or two sympathetic reviews, *The Rainbow* outraged various influential circles which set themselves up as public opinion, and was promptly banned, with the eager cooperation of the publisher.

In certain respects Lawrence's novel recalls the George Eliot of *The Mill on the Floss* and the Hardy of *Far from the Madding Crowd* and *Jude the Obscure*. The setting of the earlier part of the story is not very different geographically and socially from that of George Eliot's, while the emotional development of Ursula as a young girl, especially the transition from religious devotion to adolescent love, has something in common with Maggie Tulliver's. The account of the disastrous flood in which Tom Brangwen is drowned may also owe something to that which occurs in *The Mill on the Floss*. Similarly, we may see the spirit of Hardy in such scenes as that of the wedding feast and perhaps even in Ursula's growing disenchantment with higher education, though the latter was of course derived directly from Lawrence's own experience. A less direct but more pervasive influence on the novel is that of Emily Brontë. We sense her presence in the stress the novel often places on the relationship between the human and the natural world rather than on that between human beings and their social circumstances. The distinction between the natural and social worlds is one of the central themes of *The Rainbow* and Lawrence's handling of it is very different from anything attempted by the author of *Wuthering Heights*. But something of the atmosphere of the earlier novel is intermittently present in the later one.

The main point of citing such possible influences, however, is to bring home what a unique achievement *The Rainbow* is. The actual experience of reading it is quite unlike the experience of reading any other novel; it is not even very much like reading any other Lawrence novel. As Lawrence himself wrote:

> It is *very* different from *Sons and Lovers* : written in another language almost ... I shan't write in the same manner as *Sons and Lovers* again, I think – in that hard, violent style full of sensation and presentation.
>
> To Edward Garnett, 30 December 1913.

THE RAINBOW

D.H. Lawrence

Jacket illustration for the first edition of The Rainbow. *The accompanying blurb (possibly written by Lawrence himself) described the heroine at the close as 'waiting at the advance post, of our time to blaze a path into the future'.*

And although *Women in Love* is ostensibly a sequel, both its tone and milieu are literally worlds away from those of the earlier novel. In Richard Aldington's words, *The Rainbow* has

> a serenity and leisureliness which are absent from his first three novels and did not survive the First World War and the persecution inflicted on him for writing this literary masterpiece.

Story and fable: the biblical framework

The Rainbow is an impressive fictional interpretation of a part of English social and cultural history over three generations, roughly from the 1840s to the second decade of the twentieth century. Dr Leavis has praised this aspect of the novel and shown how Lawrence is here the true inheritor of George Eliot, particularly the George Eliot of *Middlemarch*. But Lawrence's novel is also, in intention at least, something more than imaginative social history. It aspires to the condition of myth: that is, it attempts to capture the essential rhythm of human experience not only in relation to fact and history, but in a larger relation to a trans-temporal order of being. This sounds portentous, but it is this latter ambition which imparts much of its distinctive quality to *The Rainbow*, and in attempting to fulfil it Lawrence more or less consciously casts the novel into the framework of a modern Genesis myth. The parallels between Lawrence's novel and biblical myth exists at many levels, from the structural to the stylistic. Perhaps the most obvious link is that suggested by the title. In the Old Testament the rainbow is a sign of the covenant God makes with Noah, a natural emblem of a supernatural bond. In Lawrence too the rainbow occurs at various key points in the novel, always with the suggestion of a two-way relationship, a bond between man and woman, or man and the world about him, or man and the larger non-human scheme of things. When Tom Brangwen is at a loss because of the strange mood of 'sombre exclusion' into which Lydia has fallen during her pregnancy, we are told 'He felt like a broken arch thrust sickeningly out from support.' This is perhaps the narrowest range of the symbol, whose widest occurs at the very end of the book, in Ursula's vision of the rainbow as 'the earth's new architecture . . . fitting to the over-arching heaven'.

As Tom Brangwen grows to maturity he acquires something of the stature of a biblical patriarch and his drunken speech at Anna's wedding has, paradoxically, something of prophetic dignity while at the same time faintly recalling the episode of the drunken Noah before his sons. His death reminds us that Lawrence is not simply leaning parasitically on the Genesis story in an effort to confer on his own myth a significance it does not intrinsically possess. Tom Brangwen's death indicates that the covenant is yet to be fulfilled.

The life on Marsh Farm is on the one hand presented as something valuable and concretely achieved and therefore a norm, but on the other it is also something that can never be repeated, partly because individuals differ from one another but also because the circumstances of life change from generation to generation. The flood in which Tom is carried away is presented as a vast cataclysm, an act of God recalling that in the Old Testament.

Two other aspects of the relationship between *The Rainbow* and the Old Testament go nearer the heart of the novel. Alone among Lawrence's books this one spreads itself across several generations of human history, reproducing in miniature one of the basic rhythmic patterns of the Genesis story. But it is not simply the concern with generational rather than individual time which links the novel to the Bible. It is the preoccupation in both with what may be called the theme of salvation. The manner in which the bond with God is honoured or violated is the prime reason for the recounting of individual histories in the Old Testament. In much the same way, Lawrence's real concern is not with whether a given character is successful, happy or even 'good' in the ordinary sense of these words, but ultimately with whether he or she honours or betrays the bond with life, with the deepest springs of being. In this sense *The Rainbow* can be fairly described as a religious novel.

Particular allusions to the Bible are of course frequent throughout the book and the staple of its prose is a unique and generally successful variation on the rhythms of the Authorized Version. But these gain their true significance only when we realize that the novel and the Christian scriptures are so closely related because Lawrence is trying to define in imaginative terms his own essentially religious vision of life by bringing it into an ever-changing relationship with the myths and dogmas of the religion in which, from early childhood, his consciousness has been steeped.

Repetition and variation: Lawrence's narrative method

There are two basic narrative patterns in *The Rainbow*, a linear one concerned with development in time, with one character giving place to another as a centre of interest against a background of change in milieu and circumstance, and a cyclic pattern in which each character undergoes the same struggle for fulfilment, for an adequate relationship between himself and herself and another and with the circumambient universe. In a sense each generation enacts the same story. The pattern of attraction and repulsion, the search for a meaningful relationship in life, the encounters and compromises with social reality – these are the same in outline. But in detail they are different enough for each character's particular confrontation to take on a separate significance and interest. The story expands like the widening ripples caused by a stone in water. The narrative moves out progressively from the small circle of Marsh Farm, to Cossethay and Beldover, to the larger world of school and university. In terms of time it moves from the dominantly agrarian Midlands of the early nineteenth century just before the effects of the Industrial Revolution reached it, to the realities of urban industrial living in the twentieth century as embodied in Wiggeston. But the other rhythm of what we may loosely call the characters' inner life shows a movement not towards expansion but towards concentration, as the problem of consciousness and self-consciousness becomes more acute with each passing generation.

The employment of two patterns of narration was quite deliberate on Lawrence's part. From the beginning plot had 'bored' him because he wanted to do something more than accumulate painstaking realistic detail as a background of behaviour which was psychologically plausible in a rough and ready fashion. The consequences can be felt at all levels in *The Rainbow*, in the language and its changing rhythms, in the choice and ordering of scenes and in the delineation of character. The last topic will be dealt with separately. As for Lawrence's language in the novel, he himself, as we have seen, declared that it was quite different from that of *Sons and Lovers*. In a later letter to Edward Garnett he defined the difference like this:

> I have no longer the joy in creating vivid scenes, that I had in *Sons and Lovers*, I don't care much more about accumulating objects in the powerful light of emotion, and making a scene of them. I have to write differently.

> 29 January 1914.

And he goes on to say:

> I feel that this second half of *The Sisters* is very beautiful, but it may not be sufficiently incorporated to please you.

There are some scenes in *The Rainbow* which are as vivid and as 'incorporated' as any in *Sons and Lovers* and, moreover, in the same manner. The account of Tom Brangwen's encounter with the girl at Matlock, the feeding of the cows with little Anna watching and Ursula's experiences as a schoolteacher are examples which readily come to mind. But the most characteristically vivid scenes in the novel are of a different kind. They are what Julian Moynahan in *The Deed of Life* has aptly termed ritual scenes, and include such memorable moments as that of the sheaf-gathering in the moonlight between Anna and Will, the parallel moonlight scene between Ursula and Skrebensky, Anna's naked dance and Ursula's encounter with the horses at the close. They do not belong to the linear forward-moving pattern of the narrative but rather to the cyclical pattern in which narrative time is arrested and we have little sense of before and after. And the language in which they are depicted, while it has its own kind of cumulative intensity, has also much of the hallucinatory and incantatory quality we associate with ritual. Sentences constantly circle around key words instead of moving on. Long sustained rhythmical patterns and a more than usual amount of repetition are two features of this kind of writing. Quotation would have to be lengthy to bring out these points, but the reader can easily check my comments by turning to one of the passages in question. This presumably is what Lawrence meant when he told Garnett that the style may not be 'sufficiently incorporated'. For there is a strange, disturbing disembodied quality about the writing in such passages. Simple indicative sentences referring to specific actions are usually avoided, as well as any reference to time or duration. The emphasis is invariably on inner states. Nearly always the language is heavily metaphorical and the metaphor itself often links two intangible elements rather than, as is more usual, a tangible and an intangible one. For example, just before the description of Anna's dance we are told of her that

> she must go yearning through the trouble, like a warm, glowing cloud blown in the middle of a storm.

In its context this kind of language often has great power, but it is very different indeed from the 'hard, violent style, full of sensation and presentation'.

The alternation between scenes of social documentation and everyday life and these ritualistic scenes of the inner existence makes up the narrative pattern of *The Rainbow*, though the distinction is not mechanical, as I have made it seem. The balance is heavily tipped towards ritual scenes in qualitative terms, but further discussion of these is impossible without some inquiry into Lawrence's ideas about character and motivation.

Diamond, coal and carbon: Lawrence's view of character

It was in defending a version of *The Rainbow* (then called *The Wedding Ring*) against Garnett's criticisms that Lawrence formulated one of his most famous statements of his intentions as a novelist. Garnett had objected to the psychology of the characters in the novel. 'I don't think the psychology is wrong,' replied Lawrence.

> it is only that I have a different attitude to my characters, and that necessitates a different attitude in you, which you are not prepared to give.

Thousands of readers have found that *The Rainbow* does indeed necessitate a different attitude in them from the one they usually bring to novel reading. Where exactly does the difference lie?

Once again, Lawrence himself is our most helpful guide. In the same letter he makes the following admission:

> somehow – that which is physic – non-human, in humanity, is more interesting to me than the old-fashioned human element – which causes one to conceive a character in a certain moral scheme, and make him consistent. *The certain moral scheme is what I object to.* (My italics.)
>
> Letter of 5 June 1914.

Now 'the old-fashioned human element' is exactly what the novel has traditionally concerned itself with and it is difficult to imagine how it could be otherwise. For in that phrase is contained both the notion of men and women as creatures of a definite time and place and also that of individuals as ethical beings whose attempts to adhere to or transgress against certain moral values has provided Western fiction with its *raison d'être*. This does not of course mean that the novelist merely endorses a given moral code, his own or society's. But is it possible for a novel to exist without making moral action and inter-action one of its central concerns? Let us follow Lawrence a little further on his apparently wilful path.

In the same long letter Lawrence goes on to explain his own conception of the individual:

> You mustn't look in my novel for the old stable *ego* – of the character. There is another *ego*, according to whose action the individual is unrecognisable, and passes through, as it were, allotropic states which it needs a deeper sense than any we've been used to exercise, to discover are states of the same single radically unchanged element. (Like as diamond and coal are the same pure single element of carbon. The ordinary novel would trace the history of the diamond – but I say, 'Diamond, what! This is carbon'. And my diamond might be coal or soot, and my theme is carbon.)

The dictionary tells us that allotropy is the variation of physical properties in chemicals or their compounds without change in their chemical composition. Applying the analogy to individual character, we can see that the effects of heredity and environment, of time and place, the usual determinants of character and the ordinary concern of the novelist, correspond to the variation in physical properties of a chemical element or compound. What Lawrence claims to be interested in is the unchanging chemical composition, the carbon beneath diamond, coal or soot. This raises several practical problems for the novelist, not all of which Lawrence successfully solved in *The Rainbow*.

One of the immediate problems is that characters can only express their deeper, unchanging nature by their ordinary existence, by the things they say and do in the real everyday world. But these actions and the language they speak (and the language in which the novelist renders them) are themselves the products of the socially conditioned world, the world of 'varying physical properties'. Lawrence attacks this difficulty in two main ways. In the first place he tends to reduce dialogue between characters to a bare minimum, especially in scenes of high emotional intensity. *The Rainbow* has a greater disproportion between dialogue and exposition than most twentieth-century novels. Partly this is due to the fact that Lawrence is dealing with characters who are (with the exception of Ursula) not very articulate. But the main reason is that dialogue tends to be inescapably weighted down to the social world.

When dialogue does occur, it often strikes us because of the disparity between what is said and the emotional context surrounding it. Thus in the famous sheaf-stacking scene between Will and Anna in Chapter IV, nearly four pages of powerful dramatic description are interrupted by only four brief lines of dialogue: 'We will put up some sheaves', 'You take this row', 'Put yours down' and 'No, it's your turn', before it exhausts itself in the climactic 'My love'. The inadequacy of speech is even more strongly highlighted in the prosaic words uttered by Skrebensky to Ursula at the height of their first relationship, when they kiss in the moonlight. The physical action is described by the novelist in language which draws heavily on metaphors of burning and corrosion ('She took him in the kiss, hard her kiss seized upon him, hard and fierce and burning and corrosive as the moonlight.'), but the dialogue is extremely sparse and consists of banalities such as 'Isn't it lovely?' and 'Kiss me, Anton, kiss me.'

Reducing dialogue as much as possible is one way in which Lawrence tries to remove his characters from the everyday socially-conditioned world. Another is by depicting them in scenes and situations which are at a remove from the ordinary world. It is significant that many key scenes in *The Rainbow* are set in moonlight or darkness. The man-made illumination of towns is nearly always seen as a distant and ineffectual glimmer in contrast to the fiery incandescence of moonlight or the mysterious fecundity of darkness (although the latter is occasionally overworked). Many of the most memorable scenes – the sheaf-gathering, Anna's naked dance, the cathedral scene are examples – have no immediate function as actions in everyday existence. They are really part of the symbolism of the inner life.

Another difficulty in dealing with character at its basic level of carbon is that it is very difficult to distinguish between one character and another. This is only to be expected if the novelist is primarily interested in 'that which is physic – non human, in humanity', and is what makes accounts of different characters in a state of high emotional intensity or transport very similiar and occasionally monotonous. Lawrence is to a large extent forging the vocabulary for these states and relationships as he goes along, since he has nothing in the earlier English novel to guide him (a pardonable exaggeration). He uses the language of the occult on the one hand and of science, especially electro-magnetism, on the other; in passing we may note that both these spheres are, in their different ways, far removed from ordinary living and its idiom. Sometimes the effect falls short of what Lawrence evidently intended, but most of the time the distinctive language carries power and conviction.

The final difficulty in the exploration of character at this fundamental level is that of motivation. Ordinarily we look for an explanation of a character's speech or behaviour in terms of what we understand to be his or her nature (or character!), or immediate goal or self-interest, or a combination of these, or of 'human nature' which is a series of accumulated generalizations based on collective experience. Sometimes we may delve deeper into the cloudy region of unconscious motivation. But in Lawrence's view all these, including the unconscious as usually understood, are the product of conditioning of one kind or another – 'the old-fashioned human element'. But if we go below this the ordinary sequences of motivation and action, the relation between what we say and do and why we say and do it, seems to sink to the level of the unintelligible. This often happens with Lawrentian characters and makes an added source of difficulty for the inexperienced reader. Time and again we encounter decisive changes of attitude or behaviour which are left unexplained or, which comes to the same thing, explained by epithets like 'Suddenly'. Thus when Will is at the height of his 'malignant desire' against Anna ('Anna Victrix') we read that 'Suddenly he saw that she was hurt . . . Suddenly his heart was torn with compassion for her'. Or again, for Ursula 'Skrebensky, *somehow*, had created a deadness round her, a sterility, as if the world were ashes.' ('First Love'. My italics.) Most remarkable of all, perhaps, we learn that Ursula's decision not to marry comes 'out of some far self which spoke for once beyond her'. *Pace* Lawrence, that is not the first time we have heard the voice of that far self. This latter situation is quite different from that of, say, Emma in Jane Austen's novel, who suddenly realizes towards the end that she and she alone must marry Knightley. The novelist has been dropping clues for us about this all the way, and part of our enjoyment is due to the fact that Emma takes so long to see what is so plain to us. In *The Rainbow* Ursula's decision is quite literally inexplicable in terms of what we know about her as a 'character'. But it is part of Lawrence's triumph here and elsewhere in the novel that he convinces us that there is a deeper stratum from which characters respond and that this is something more than an arbitrary figment of the novelist's imagination.

Throughout *The Rainbow* Lawrence creates characters who have, so to speak, two identities. At one level they are recognizable human beings, farmers, emigres, schoolteachers, husbands, wives, daughters and so on. But below this they are centres of consciousness and action who are both free and bound – free in being unconditioned by social or even genetic constraints (remember Lawrence's insistence on the *absolute* newness of each centre of life in *Psychoanalysis and the Unconscious*), but bound in the sense that in these deeper states they acknowledge the connection between themselves and the vast superhuman process which is life. Among its many resonances, the rainbow itself stands for the possibility of union between these two identities, a union which can never be one of causality and dependence but will always remain contingent and mysterious.

The uses of symbolism

One of the most important ways in which Lawrence convinces us of the reality of the inner non-social world to which his characters have access is by his use of symbolism. It is unnecessary and would be tedious to catalogue the various symbols used in the novel. What is perhaps worth pointing out is that Lawrence does not use symbols in an unchanging one-to-one relationship with their referments, so that all we need do is 'decode' a symbol once and for all. Rather he uses symbols in a circle of ever-widening range so that they begin to accumulate imaginative power as the novel develops. I have already contrasted two uses of the central image of the rainbow, once in a variant form as a broken arch at the opening of the novel and once at the end as the fully formed rainbow itself. In between, this dominant symbol takes on a variety of forms and meanings. Just as the broken arch stands for the defective relationship between man and woman, so the rainbow symbolizes the perfected marital state and is linked, through the common factor of the arch, to the brilliant 'Cathedral' chapter depicting Will and Anna in their wedded relationship. But here the cathedral takes on a double significance. For Will it is an image of the perfect consummation of man, beyond time and death:

> Spanned round with the rainbow, the jewelled gloom folded music upon silence, light upon darkness, fecundity upon death, as a seed folds leaf upon leaf and silence upon the root and the flower, hushing up the secret of all between its parts, the death out of which it fell, the life into which it has dropped, the immortality it involves, and the death it will embrace again.

Anna, however, denies the finality and inhuman perfection of the cathedral. She at once keeps her feet firmly on the ground (in her insistence on the realism of the little carved faces) and soars above the span of the cathedral arch, in denying the consummation represented by the altar. But the novel does not at this point ask us to take sides as between Will and Anna.

The rainbow also symbolizes the self liberated from the petty constraints of acquisitive social living as well as, in the final vision, human life itself transfigured, though Ursula's vision has a kind of detachable quality to it, as if it did not quite arise out of what has gone before. But we should not make too much of this. Perhaps we should see it in conjunction with the image of the horses which precedes it as two sides of the same coin, a reminder of the sinister destructive power of the dark forces of life as well as of their creative potentiality.

Apart from the related symbolism of rainbow arch and cathedral and that of the stampeding horses, there are also the symbolic or ritual scenes already discussed as well as occasional symbolic characters such as the bargeman and his wife and the cabman with the animal-like face who drives Ursula and Skrebensky to their London hotel. Such characters fit in perfectly well at the narrative level but their true importance lies in the way they fill out our understanding of the novel's theme at these points. In a similar way, the use of the natural scene – clouds, a stormy moonlit sky, darkness – in the first chapter is quite realistic but also serves as a metaphor for the strange blend of nearness and apartness, force and tenderness in the relationship between Tom and Lydia. The use of moonlight and the moon itself in the scenes involving Ursula and Skrebensky is somewhat different, for here the moon is often treated not so much as a symbol of non-human energy as a source of it, a feature which reappears in *Women in Love*. Perhaps it is not altogether irrelevant to recall a passage in which Jessie Chambers describes a walk by moonlight with Lawrence:

> In the evening he and I wandered along the beach waiting to see the moon rise over the sea. We set off light-heartedly enough, but gradually some dark power seemed to take possession of Lawrence, and when the final beauty of the moonrise broke upon us, something seemed to explode inside him. I cannot remember now what he said, but his words were wild, and he appeared to be in great distress of mind, and possibly also of body.

For a novelist as passionately convinced as Lawrence of the interconnectedness of human and non-human life, symbolism could never really be anything as simple as a 'fictional' nature standing for a 'real' human aspect; if anything, the situation was often likely to be the reverse, reminding us once again of Lawrence's interest in 'that which is physic – non-human, in humanity'. 'Physic' comes from a Greek word meaning, among other things, 'nature'.

The novelist and the preacher

There is very little point in objecting that Lawrence the preacher gets in the way of Lawrence the novelist to the latter's detriment. With the exception of his first three books, all Lawrence's novels are firmly and unashamedly didactic in intent. Lawrence valued the form of the novel precisely because it was better suited to preaching than, say, the sermon. The sermon speaks with one voice, the voice of the preacher. But the novel speaks not only with the novelist's voice, but with its own, independent of his – 'Never trust the artist, trust the tale.' In fact, as Lawrence insisted, the good novel always contains an implicit criticism of the author's morality.

Thus didacticism in *The Rainbow* is not simply a matter of preaching a Lawrentian morality to supplant the Christian morality which Lawrence outgrew but to which he kept returning. Rather it is a matter, to quote Lawrence again, of 'the way our sympathy flows and recoils'. If this is what 'really determines our lives', then

> here lies the vast importance of the novel, properly handled. It can inform and lead into new places the flow of our sympathetic consciousness and it can lead our sympathy away in recoil from things gone dead.
>
> *Lady Chatterley's Lover* (Ch. IX)

This is far removed from what we usually understand by didacticism or preaching. But for all that it is a kind of teaching, and Lawrence is fully committed to it in *The Rainbow*. I believe that the balance between the teacher and the novelist (if that is not a misleading way of putting it) is maintained better in this novel than in any of his others. It consists in part of the way in which Lawrence succeeds both in entering into a character's consciousness and yet remaining partly outside it. This enables him to make the miraculously fluent transitions from one figure to the next as the centre of interest in the evolving narrative. Equally important (perhaps it is only another way of making the same point) is the way in which authorial comment always seems to do full justice to a given character without detracting from the force of another character's opposed outlook. The exception to this is Skrebensky, who is too often used as a stalking horse by Ursula. But there is another Skrebensky with something of Ursula's own demonic power who emerges in the novel in spite of Ursula. Elsewhere we really do feel 'the flow of our sympathetic consciousness' being led into truly new places, sometimes fearful ones. Finally, we nearly always feel that the comment arises naturally out of the given circumstances, and only very rarely that the latter are manipulated in order to provide a setting for the former (as for instance in the undemonstrated assertion that 'The college itself was a little slovenly laboratory for the factory'). Tom Brangwen's speech at the wedding feast is a good and representative example of the way the novelist and the teacher work in close harmony in *The Rainbow*.

Lawrence's sense of an ending

Many readers have found the ending of *The Rainbow* unsatisfactory. I have already mentioned its 'detachable' quality in relation to what has gone before. F. R. Leavis considers that by the time he came to write the ending, Lawrence had already passed beyond the radically optimistic mood in which the book's central symbol was conceived. If so, the ending itself becomes one of the ways in which the novel constitutes a criticism of the author's morality. The fact that *The Rainbow* was created out of materials that were not wholly used up in its making also partly accounts for its special character; there is more of the story of these characters, especially Ursula's and Gudrun's, yet to be told. There is also the question of at what level the novel is to be concluded. As an unfolding story of three generations of English life *The Rainbow* is satisfying enough and its ending, with the young Ursula poised on the threshold of life in the industrial–metropolitan world, is convincing in its very tentativeness. Similarly, as part of Ursula's emotional education, her encounters with Skrebensky and Miss Inger are persuasive. On the other hand, as the record of the subterranean ebb and flow of psychic feeling among the principal characters, it is difficult to see how the book could have an ending in the ordinary sense (unless in some impossible 'ideal' union) since this pattern, as I have remarked, is circular rather than linear. The added complication that, with Ursula, Lawrence is entering into the area of his own period and experience is also present. But what is perhaps least convincing about the final paragraph of the novel is the too-easy assimilation of what had just before been called 'corruption triumphant and unopposed, corruption so pure that it is hard and brittle' into the new vision in which even the corruption has a redeeming quality:

> And the rainbow stood on the earth. She knew that the sordid people who crept hard-scaled and separate on the face of the world's corruption were living still, that the rainbow was arched in their blood and would quiver to life in their spirit, that they would cast off their horny covering of disintegration . . . She saw in the rainbow the earth's new architecture, the old, brittle corruption of houses and factories swept away . . .

It is not the element of wish-fulfilment, which is perfectly appropriate in a vision, to which one may object here but the glibness with which 'the old, brittle corruption', so powerfully embodied in Wiggeston and elsewhere, is so tidily 'swept away' and the hard brittleness of absolute corruption becomes merely the horny covering which conceals a new life. In overtly political terms, *The Rainbow* is certainly a revolutionary novel, and we may, if we wish, link this final vision to Ursula's earlier desire that 'her soul's action should be the smashing of the great machine.' (Ch. XII) But there is an unsettling glibness about it all the same.

As a novel, *The Rainbow* has many of the defects one would expect in a pioneering work – overwriting, uncertainty of tone, occasional blurring of focus and an ending which is in some ways unsatisfactory. But with all its faults, the novel continues to prove more vitally and lastingly interesting to generations of readers than many a well made work held up to Lawrence for emulation. We may leave it with a final comment from the author himself:

> Tell Arnold Bennett that all rules of construction hold good only for novels which are copies of other novels. A book which is not a copy of other books has its own construction, and what he calls faults, he being an old imitator, I call characteristics. I shall repeat it till I am grey – when they have as good a work to show, they may make their pronouncements *ex cathedra*. Till then, let them learn decent respect.
>
> Still, I think he's generous.

Letter to J. B. Pinker, 16 December 1915.

6 *Women in Love*

Many critics consider *Women in Love* to be Lawrence's greatest novel. There is no room here to do anything like justice to its originality and power. Two very perceptive accounts of it, written from widely different standpoints, are by F. R. Leavis in his book *D. H. Lawrence: Novelist* and by Colin Clarke in *River of Dissolution*. All I wish to do is to comment very briefly on the relationship between *The Rainbow* and *Women in Love*.

Ursula and Gudrun are, as we know, the central figures of *Women in Love*, along with Rupert Birkin and Gerald Crich. The presence of the two sisters provides one kind of continuity between the two novels, as does the reappearance of characters such as Will Brangwen. A more important link is that between Ursula's search for a meaningful life in the modern world and the continuation of that quest in *Women in Love* in the wider and more troubled arena of the metropolitan–industrial world as well as that of the survivals of the rural past. There is greater cognizance of the social world in *Women in Love*, but the same insistence as in the earlier work that the psychic ebb and flow within a human being and between human beings, insofar as it links them with the larger processes of life, is the crucial factor governing psychological well-being as well as social sanity. For Lawrence, though not for Marx, consciousness as he defined it determined social existence.

All this makes the two novels sound much more alike than they really are. The major differences between them – differences of emphasis, tone and direction – can be attributed to the war and to Lawrence's experiences during this period. The bulk of what became *The Rainbow* was finished before the war, while *Women in Love* was extensively rewritten during the war years and was not eventually published till 1920. As Lawrence himself explained in a letter written to Waldo Frank in July 1917:

> About *The Rainbow*: it was all written before the war, though revised during Sept. and Oct. of 1914. I don't think the war had much to do with it – I don't think the war altered it, from its pre-war statement. I only clarified a little, in revision. I knew I was writing a destructive work, otherwise I couldn't have called it *The Rainbow* – in reference to the Flood ... And I knew, as I revised the book, that it was a kind of working up to the dark sensual or Dionysic or Aphrodisic ecstasy, which does actually burst the world-consciousness in every individual.

But though he here calls *The Rainbow* 'a destructive work' the very title suggests it is more than that and the experience of reading the novel amply confirms this. Lawrence's letter continues:

> There is another novel, sequel to *The Rainbow*, called *Women in Love* ... This actually does contain the results in one's soul of the war: *it is purely destructive, not like* 'The Rainbow,' *destructive-consummating*. (My italics.)

With his usual critical acuteness, Lawrence here puts his finger on the essential connection as well as the essential difference between the two novels. There *is* a strong destructive impulse in *The Rainbow* and it is certainly not always sharply distinguished from the creative or life-enhancing forces, for example in the association of Ursula with the corrosive-burning energies of the moon. But this destructive energy is much more sharply emphasized in the later novel, and its ambiguous nature much more insistently evoked by Lawrence's metaphorical language. *Women in Love* is a novel which gains some of its power from the conflict within it of opposing impulses – the impulse to exult in the coming apocalyptic destruction and the impulse to preach the last desperate message of salvation. It is a more difficult book to read than *The Rainbow* and a much more disturbing one, not easily to be comprehended within a life-enhancing morality alone despite Dr Leavis's finest efforts. To give the last word to Lawrence: 'One may know a new utterance by the element of danger in it.'

7 The shorter fiction

As in all his work, what strikes one most when one comes to Lawrence's shorter fiction is the enormous variety within it. The three volumes of *Complete Short Stories* in the Phoenix edition contain forty-seven stories but do not include the longer tales such as 'St Mawr', 'The Escaped Cock', 'The Virgin and the Gipsy' and many others. And it is not only in length that the tales vary. Their raw material ranges from the life of working class folk in the Midlands of Lawrence's childhood to the fashionable cosmopolitan circle of literary expatriates in America and on the continent. A few of the stories, among which 'The Rocking-Horse Winner' is the best, dabble in the supernatural, while others, such as 'Smile', hover uneasily on its edge. The narrative tone of the stories is also very wide-ranging. Sometimes, as in many of the early stories with a Midland setting, it is that of a keen yet sympathetic chronicler; elsewhere Lawrence uses a tone of satirical banter and again there is a harsher, bitterer tone as in 'New Eve and Old Adam', a story about a newly married couple who separate briefly because she is dissatisfied, come together in intense passion and part again with mutual recriminations. Lawrence also experiments with different kinds of narrative technique, including the first person narrator, the impersonal and omniscient narrator and the narrator who is himself a participant in the story.

Lawrence's earliest published work was the short story, 'A Prelude', which he entered under Jessie Chambers' name for a Christmas competition in a Nottingham newspaper. Throughout his life he continued to write short fiction. The relationship of these to his major novels varies with different stories. Most of his early short stories were collected in two volumes, *The Prussian Officer*, published in 1914 and *A Modern Lover*, posthumously published in 1934. The themes and settings of many of these stories are very similar to those of *The White Peacock* and *Sons and Lovers* and some of them, in a different form, probably became part of those novels. 'Her Turn', 'Strike Pay' and 'Odour of Chrysanthemums', among several others, convey the atmosphere of the mining community. But the title story in *The Prussian Officer* is a powerful evocation of the relationship between an infantry captain and his peasant orderly. It was probably suggested by Lawrence's first visit to Frieda's home town in Germany. The relation between discipline and unacknowledged passion is vividly suggested and there is a brilliant counterpoint between the hypnotic rhythm of attraction and repulsion between the two men and the utter stillness of the heat-haze in which much of the action takes place. Thus in his very first volume of short stories Lawrence gives us one of his finest pieces of writing, although it was one which he revised extensively since its first magazine publication.

The stories in the collection entitled *England My England* (published 1922) date from the war years and are loosely connected with *The Rainbow* and *Women in Love*. For instance, the sense of the father's gradual exclusion from his wife's emotional circle after the birth of their children, which is the main theme of the title story, links it with the early part of *The Rainbow*, though the remarkable final section, describing the hero's death, is quite new and is a unique feat of imagination for one who was not an active combatant.

The following year saw the publication of a volume containing three long tales, 'The Ladybird', 'The Fox' and 'The Captain's Doll'. The latter two are acknowledged as two of Lawrence's masterpieces of short fiction and are illuminatingly discussed by Dr Leavis. Dr Leavis' discussion of 'St Mawr', which belongs to Lawrence's Mexican period, is also deservedly well known. To this group too belongs 'The Princess' (together with which *St Mawr* was first published in book form) and 'The Woman Who Rode Away'. In many respects the latter is more compact and therefore a more satisfactory rendering of a major theme of *The Plumed Serpent* – the search of a modern Western woman for her true roots in an older culture – without most of the unassimilated preaching which disfigures the novel.

When Lawrence returned to Europe for the last time, he knew he was a dying man, but paradoxically that knowledge produced some of his finest writing in celebration of the ceaseless miracle of life, both in poetry and in his short stories. Shortly before that, however, he vented his bitterness and frustration at the petty-minded officialdom which had succeeded in censoring his books and closing the exhibition of his paintings in the snarling little *Pansies* and *Nettles* as well as in sardonic short stories such as 'The Lovely Lady'. In this last phase Lawrence also wrote a long tale which is in many ways unique in his fiction and is at the opposite end of the narrative spectrum from the realism of an early masterpiece like 'Odour of Chrysanthemums'. This is the story called 'The Escaped Cock', later published in a longer version as 'The Man Who Died' (the later title apparently does not have Lawrence's authority). I have chosen these two stories for further comment.

'Odour of Chrysanthemums'

This story, which is based on material which Lawrence was to use for his play *The Widowing of Mrs Holroyd* and again for one of his fine dialect poems, exists in four separate versions. It originally appeared in the *English Review* in June 1911. A later version was included in *The Prussian Officer* (1914). But some years ago there came to light a

JIX, THE SELF-APPOINTED CHUCKER-OUT.

(LEFT TO RIGHT)
A "FRANK" WOMAN NOVELIST, SHAKESPERE, SHAW, WELLS, BENNETT, ALDOUS HUXLEY,
D. H. LAWRENCE, JAMES JOYCE. EACH IS ACCOMPANIED BY HIS LITERARY INSPIRATION.

(AT BACK) DICKENS AND JANE AUSTEN

set of printer's proofs of the story together with Lawrence's extensive revisions and manuscript additions. My discussion relates to the final version, as reprinted in the three-volume *Complete Short Stories*.

'Poetic realism' would do as well as any single phrase to describe the mode of this fine story. The situation it deals with is perfectly realistic and a very familiar one in a mining community. It is that of a miner who dies in an accident at the pit and whose corpse is brought home to the waiting wife and family. But Lawrence handles the familiar matter in an unexpected and illuminating way. The opening paragraph, which describes a locomotive engine passing by while an anonymous woman watches it, introduces us to the familiar milieu of the industrialized landscape in which industry has so far not quite extinguished the natural environment. The colt which is startled from the gorse by the noise of the train still 'outdistanced it at a canter'. The paragraph ends with a reminder of the source of both the livelihood of the community and the pollution of its environment:

> The pit-bank looked up beyond the pond, flames like red sores licking its ashy sides, in the afternoon's stagnant light. Just beyond rose the tapering chimneys and the clumsy black headstocks of Brinsley Colliery.

Then there is a brief glimpse of miners returning home in the raw evening before we are introduced both to one of the central images of the story – 'Beside the path hung dishevelled pink chrysanthemums' – and the central character – 'a tall woman of imperious mien, handsome, with definite black eyebrows'. From her conversation with her child we gain an insight into her domineering character and her pretensions to gentility ('Don't do that – it does look nasty', she tells the boy who is scattering chrysanthemum petals on the path). We also learn that she is the daughter of the engine-driver, and therefore a native of the community. Thus marriage to the miner has something of the character of inevitable female destiny, an important minor theme in the story. The brief exchange between father and daughter about the former's remarriage focuses our attention on the crucial importance of marriage in this society, and how it is very much a male-oriented institution. 'Well, what's a man to do?', asks the father. 'It's no sort of life for a man of my years, to sit at my own hearth like a stranger.'

Then we are in the small kitchen, the table laid expectantly for tea, the fire brightly glowing, then sinking as the time passes and the father has not yet returned. The men trooping home get fewer and fewer, the daughter returns home from school and is duly chided

Low's cartoon about the seizing of Lady Chatterley's Lover *by the police. "Jix" was Sir William Joynson-Hicks, then Home Secretary. The comment in longhand is by Lawrence.*

for being late, and still there is no sign of the man of the house. The family sits down to tea without him, the mother complains that he is probably at the public house as usual, the lamps are lit, and once again the image of chrysanthemums enters the narrative though without any feeling of being forced into symbolic significance. The daughter notices a chrysanthemum at her mother's apron and wants to smell it, reminding the mother of her own associations with the bloom:

'Don't they smell beautiful?'
Her mother gave a short laugh.
'No', she said, 'not to me. It was chrysanthemums when I married him, chrysanthemums when you were born, and the first time they ever brought him home drunk, he'd got brown chrysanthemums in his buttonhole.'

Thus unobtrusively and wholly naturally the flower becomes associated with the pattern of the woman's life, while the detail about the chrysanthemums in the man's buttonhole when he was first brought home drunk perhaps sets up a faint menacing hint of what is to come. There is a kind of prospective irony in the contrast between the growing anger of the wife at what she believes to be her husband's selfish merrymaking and the reader's growing awareness that something other than drinking is making the man late. But Lawrence is not particularly concerned to enforce this irony. When the children have been packed off to bed and the mother comes down again to wait for her husband, we are told: 'Meantime her anger was tinged with fear.'

The tension is further increased when the woman goes to a neighbour's to inquire after her husband and is told that when last seen he was still at work in the pit, even after it was time to leave. There is also an apparently unrelated detail which heightens our suspense when the neighbour warns the woman to mind her step in the dark – '"Ah've said many a time as Ah'd fill up them ruts in this entry, sym'dy'll be breaking their legs yit."'

While the neighbour goes in search of the miner, the wife settles down to wait again. She is joined by her mother-in-law and her very first words suggest some impending tragedy, though she has no definite news. '"Eh Lizzie, whatever shall we do, whatever shall we do?"', she asks, but in answer to her daughter-in-law's inquiry '"What is it mother?"' can only reply '"I don't know, child, I can't tell you."' But her premonition prompts the wife to ask the question she dreads: '"Is he dead?"'

So far the narrative has been almost wholly realistic, with the symbolic overtones of the flowers completely absorbed into the realistic treatment. With the arrival of miners bringing in the husband's dead body, the narrative takes on a more ritualistic and elegiac quality. The transition is beautifully effected by the older woman's blend of reminiscence and premonition. Once again we are offered, through the wife's eyes, a glimpse of chrysanthemums, and for the first time they are specifically associated with death: 'There was a cold, deathly smell of chrysanthemums in the room.'

Lawrence's treatment of the final stages of the story has a lot in common with J. M. Synge's masterly handling of a similar situation in his short play *Riders to the Sea*. There is the same humble setting, the same situation of sudden death and its impact on the family, the same sense of ritual and dignity which lifts domestic tragedy into a loftier, more impersonal plane. Here, as she washes the body of her dead husband and prepares it for burial, the newly made widow realizes three things to the full: first, the utter remoteness and separateness of the man who was lately her husband from her. 'She saw him, how utterly inviolable he lay in himself.' Secondly, she becomes aware of her failure to make any real vital relationship with her husband when he was alive. 'There had been nothing between them, and yet they had come together, exchanging their nakedness repeatedly.' The mother's lamentations over her dead son only serve to highlight the sheer emptiness of the marriage relationship. Finally, the wife comes to realize the utter aloneness of her new life – 'Her life was gone like this.' But the awareness gives her a kind of stoic strength to accept life. By a profound but familiar paradox, the intimate acquaintance with death, though unnerving, becomes a means to a richer recognition of life's possibilities, however meagre: 'She knew she submitted to life, which was her immediate master. But from death, her ultimate master, she winced with fear and shame.'

'*The Escaped Cock*'/'*The Man Who Died*'

Where 'Odour of Chrysanthemums' dwells on the dignity and inviolability of death, 'The Escaped Cock' takes as its theme the beauty and mystery of life here and now. The immediate occasion of the story – the sight of a toy cockbird escaping from its egg in a shop window – has already been noted. In a letter to his American friend Earl Brewster Lawrence commented:

> I wrote a story of the Resurrection, where Jesus gets up and feels very sick about everything, and can't stand the old crowd any more – so cuts out – and as he heals up, he begins to find out what an astonishing place the phenomenal world is, far more marvellous than any salvation or heaven – and thanks his stars he needn't have a 'mission' any more. It's called *The Escaped Cock* from that toy in Volterra. Do you remember?

But Lawrence was by no means the first writer of the time to attempt a refashioning of the Christian story. Ever since the great intellectual upheavals of the nineteenth century associated with such names as Lyell, Darwin and Huxley, the revaluation and reinterpretation of Christian myth and dogma had occupied many thinkers and artists. Among the latter were Oscar Wilde, Samuel Butler and George Moore, each of whom tried his hand at recasting the Christ story. With all their differences, these reshapings share the common feature that they all tend to humanize Christ. In addition, George Moore's *The Brook Kerith* (1916) fits Lawrence's summary of his own short story very neatly too.

What Lawrence's rather slangy remarks totally fail to convey is the extraordinary poetic quality of the style in which he wrote his story. It is a style which has all the radiant clarity of the best of his last poems and the evocative power of *Apocalypse* to which phase of his writing it belongs. It blends realism with a mythic quality in a manner very characteristic of poems such as 'The Man of Tyre'. It recalls Lawrence's statement in *Apocalypse* that it is myth which 'reaches the deep emotional centres every time'. Here is a description of the central figure, the Man who died, confronting the world immediately on his resurrection:

> Having nowhere to go, he turned away from the city that stood on her hills. He slowly followed the road away from the town, past the olives, under which purple anemones were drooping in the chill of dawn, and rich-green herbage was pressing thick. The world, the same as ever, the natural world, thronging with greenness, a nightingale winsomely, wistfully, coaxingly calling from the bushes beside a runnel of water, in the world, the natural world of morning and evening, forever undying, from which he had died.

The rhythm of the last sentence, with its repetition of 'the world' and its flashing images of greenness, bird song and falling water, so beautifully captures the wonder and freshness of created things that we hardly notice that according to the grammar book it is hardly a sentence; and when we do notice we hardly care. Only very rarely does the repetition become tedious and mechanical.

The first part of the story concerns the resurrected man's re-acquaintance with the world, his repudiation of his spiritual mission as a Messiah and his acceptance of the limits and splendours of the flesh. These developments are signified by a series of events, the most important of which is the releasing by the man of a cock which a boorish peasant has tied by the leg. The cock is a sort of activated pun, and the bird itself fades out of the story once the carnal vigour which it represents is slowly realized in the man himself. Through his awareness of a peasant woman's desire for him, even though he cannot reciprocate it, he comes to a realization of the supreme importance of life in the flesh. He rejects Mary Magdalene's homage and through her his own former goal of spiritual salvation. The first part ends with the resurrected man sick of the world's mania to lay a spiritual compulsion on men, as he had wished to do:

> And he thought of his own mission, how he had tried to lay the compulsion of love on all men. And the old nausea came back on him. For there was no contact without a subtle attempt to inflict a compulsion. And already he had been compelled even into death. The nausea of the old wound broke out afresh, and he looked again on the world with repulsion, dreading its mean contacts.

In the second part of the story the incantatory style is heightened and the atmosphere of myth rather than individual history is more pronounced. Here Lawrence boldly brings the Christian resurrection myth in contact with a far older one, the Egyptian myth of Osiris, slain by his jealous brother Set and finally found by his sister-wife Isis and enthroned as Lord of the Underworld and Ruler of the Dead. Lawrence would have been familiar with this myth in all its details from his reading of J. G. Frazer's monumental study *The Golden Bough*.

The climax of the second part is the union between Isis seeking her dead husband and the resurrected man. When he lies with her he awakens once more in his own body and this fulfilment is Lawrence's own version of the Christian story. For the tragic sacrifice of the Christian myth he substitutes the ecstatic affirmation of his own. As she soothes his scars with oil, desire slowly wells up within him and rises to a pitch that takes him beyond himself – 'Now I am not myself – I am something new' till the consciousness of the woman becomes transcendent:

> He quivered, as the sun burst up in his body. Stooping, he laid his hand softly on her warm bright shoulder, and the shock of desire went through him, shock after shock, so that he wondered if it were another sort of death. But full of magnificence.
> Now all his consciousness was there in the crouching, hidden woman. He stopped beside her and caressed her softly, blindly, murmuring inarticulate things. And his death and his passion of sacrifice were all as nothing to him now, he knew only the crouching fulness of the woman, there, the soft white rock of life.

Clearly it is not merely sexual union as the term is usually understood which is being celebrated here. The two figures, by this point in the story, have gained a mythic stature which makes them more than two individuals. Behind them resonate two versions of one of the most powerful myths in human culture. Furthermore, the union between the man and the woman is presented, in a characteristically Lawrentian fashion, as embodying a right relationship between humanity and the non-human forces of life, which we neglect at our peril:

But the man looked at the vivid stars before dawn, as they rained down to the sea, and the dog-star green towards the sea's rim. And he thought: How plastic it is, how full of curves and folds like an invisible rose of dark-petalled openness, that shows where dew touches its darkness. How full it is, and great beyond all gods. How it leans around me, and I am part of it, the great rose of space. I am like a grain of its perfume, and the woman is a grain of its beauty. Now the world is one flower of many-petalled darknesses, and I am in its perfume as in a touch.

Sexual and natural imagery are inextricably intertwined here. Each is a metaphor of the other, for it is their inter-involvement which the story embodies.

But the sexual fulfilment is not the point at which the story ends. The man who died finally leaves the woman, she carrying his seed within her, he strengthened by his fleshly contact with her – 'I carry her perfume in my flesh like essence of roses.' He sets sail alone towards a new day and a new resurrected world.

'The Escaped Cock', like many of Lawrence's writings, exists in several versions. It has been carefully edited by Gerald M. Lacy and published as a separate volume (1973) by the Black Sparrow Press, with a full discussion of the various versions. Perhaps the best commentary on what Lawrence was trying to achieve in the story is one of his own essays, 'The Risen Lord' (published in *Assorted Articles*), which one critic has called a 'third part' of 'The Escaped Cock'. In that essay Lawrence, starting from the assumption that 'the great religious images are only images of our own experiences, or of our own state of mind and soul', goes on to assert that neither the image of Christ crucified, which the Church so busily and partially propagates nor the sentimental image of the Madonna and Child, which had been blasted to extinction by the guns of the First World War, are adequate religious images for modern man. What he sees as the great need, which he triumphantly fulfils in imaginative terms in the tale, is the restoration of the image of Christ risen in the flesh, in the world in which we all live and die. A few lines from the essay may serve as a fitting epigraph to this most beautiful of all Lawrence's stories:

Christ risen in the flesh! We must accept the image complete, if we accept it at all. We must take the mystery in its fulness and in fact. It is only the image of our own experience. Christ rises, when he rises from the dead, in the flesh, not merely as spirit. He rises with hands and feet, as Thomas knew for certain: and if with hands and feet, then with lips and stomach and genitals of a man. Christ risen, and risen in the whole of his flesh, not with some left out . . .

... If Jesus rose as a full man, in full flesh and soul, then He rose to take a woman to Himself, to live with her, and to know the tenderness and blossoming of his twoness with her ... If Jesus rose in the full flesh, He rose to know the tenderness of a woman, and the great pleasure of her, and to have children by her.

8 Lawrence's poetry

The fact that Lawrence is without question a great poetic novelist has had the unfortunate effect that his poetry has been either neglected, patronized or dismissed. With the exception of anthology pieces such as 'Snake' and 'Piano' very few of Lawrence's poems are anything like as well known as they deserve to be. He himself noted this fact with some annoyance. 'In England,' he wrote to a Croydon friend in 1914, 'people have got that loathsome superior knack of refusing to consider me a poet at all.' 'Your prose is so good', say the kind fools, 'that we are obliged to forgive you your poetry. How I hate them.' In 1914, Lawrence had published only one book of poems, *Love Poems and Others*. By the end of his life he had added nine more volumes, so that we have far less excuse to neglect his poetry than those reviewers and critics who were writing at the outset of Lawrence's career. This brief survey of his poetry may aptly begin by noting that he was writing verse before he was quite out of his teens and continued to do so until his death. In his Introduction to the *Collected Poems* of 1928 Lawrence wrote:

> The first poems I ever wrote, if poems they were, was when I was nineteen: now twenty three years ago. I remember perfectly the Sunday afternoon when I perpetrated those first two pieces: 'To Guelder Roses' and 'To Campions'; in spring-time, of course, and, as I say, in my twentieth year. Any young lady might have written them and been pleased with them; as I was pleased with them.

As usual, Lawrence is very perceptive about his own work. These poems as well as many others of this period are indeed pretty maidenly effusions full of consciously 'poetical' phrases such as 'the purple dreams of the innocent spring', and 'preaching in sad-moving silence a heart-hungry purity'. The ghostly hand of Dowson and the Pre-Raphaelites almost extinguishes whatever life and individual spirit they may have. Almost, but not quite, for even in these very earliest efforts we have the characteristic Lawrentian theme of the waste of ingrown virginity expressed in the contrast between the campions which

> Draw nearer, redden and laugh like young girls kissed
> into a daring, short-breath'd confession . . .
> and the guelder roses

> Such pearléd zones of fair sterility
> Girdling with jewels the meanness of common things.

Most of these early poems are autobiographical both in their subject matter and their setting. They deal with the torment and tenderness of awakening love, and particularly with the difficult relationship between Jessie Chambers and the young Lawrence. The background is usually Haggs Farm or Eastwood, nostalgically evoked during the Croydon period. To this period too belong a group of poignant poems dealing with the death of Lawrence's mother, and a few remarkable poems in the Midlands dialect, such as 'Violets' and 'Whether or Not' which combine dramatic power, psychological insight and touches of humour in a uniquely Lawrentian manner. One of the most characteristic and successful of the early poems, which draws on nostalgia, adolescent love and a distinctive version of the pathetic fallacy, is 'Renascence'.

Renascence

We have bit no forbidden apple,
    Eve and I,
Yet the splashes of day and night
Falling around us, no longer dapple
The same valley with purple and white.

This is our own still valley,
    Our Eden, our home;
But day shows it vivid with feeling
And the pallor of night does not tally
With dark sleep that once covered the ceiling.

The little red heifer: tonight I looked in her eyes;
    She will calve tomorrow.
Last night, when I went with the lantern, the sow was grabbing
    her litter
With snarling red jaws; and I heard the cries
Of the new-born, and then, the old owl, then the bats that flitter.

And I woke to the sound of the wood-pigeon and lay and listened
    Till I could borrow
A few quick beats from a wood-pigeon's heart; and when I did rise
Saw where the morning sun on the shaken iris glistened.
And I knew that home, this valley, was wider than Paradise.

I learned it all from my Eve,
    The warm, dumb wisdom;
She's a quicker instructress than years;
She has quickened my pulse to receive
Strange throbs, beyond laughter and tears.

So now I know the valley
    Fleshed all like me

With feelings that change and quiver
And clash, and yet seem to tally,
Like all the clash of a river
    Moves on to the sea.

This poem, in a slightly different form, was first published in *Love
Poems and Others* (1913) and while it is weighted down with the
influence of Hardy and the Meredith of 'Love in the Valley' a good
deal of Lawrence's individual voice comes through. As a 'nature
poem' it is much more alive and sparkling than the pallidly genteel
landscapes which were all that most Georgian poets could make out
of their response to nature. While the apple/dapple rhyme may set
off uncomfortable echoes of Drinkwater, the second stanza, with its
awkward rhyming, nevertheless alerts us to the fact that this is not
just a 'nature poem' – something is happening in this landscape. All
Lawrence's nature poems are landscapes with figures, even if the
figure is only that of the perceiving poet. The connection between
the speaker's own identity and emotion is made explicit in

        So now I know the valley
        Fleshed all like me

But the bare, vigorous assertiveness of those lines has been earned by
the earlier stanzas about the calving heifer and the identification
between the speaker's heart-beats and wood-pigeon's. The close
and realistic observation of the scene in the heifer's stall with its hint
of menace – 'snarling red jaws' – saves the succeeding lines about the
wood-pigeon from sentimentality and lead on to the incandescent
lyricism of

    Saw where the morning sun on the shaken iris glistened
    And I knew that home, this valley, was wider than Paradise,

The poem is of course shot through with nostalgic recollections, but
it is a nostalgia almost as finely controlled as in the deservedly
famous 'Piano'. One of the most remarkable features in it is the
handling of rhyme and metre. In Lawrence, as in Hardy, rhyme is
often awkward, but as with the older poet, the very awkwardness
sometimes becomes a kind of strength, a sign of an individual and
independent vision. Perhaps that does not quite happen here, though
feminine rhymes, such as 'listened/glistened' and 'litter/flitter' are
effectively used. But whatever uncertainty there may be in the
handling of rhyme, that of metre is subtle and striking. Formally,
Lawrence uses a rhymed five-line stanza, yet within it he manages
to retain all the directness of urgent utterance. And while the rhyme-
scheme and the metrical form are stable throughout, Lawrence has
no time at all for the counting-on-the-fingers approach to metre.
This was one of the many points of conflict between him and Edward

Marsh who published some of Lawrence's early verse in *Georgian Poetry* and was a valued patron and friend. 'I always wonder if the Greeks and Romans really did scan', he wrote in a letter of 1913 to Marsh, 'or, if scansion wasn't a thing invented afterwards by the schoolmaster.' Earlier in the same letter he had written

> I think I read my poetry more by length than by stress – as a matter of movements in space than footsteps hitting the earth . . . I think more of a bird with broad wings flying and lapsing through the air, than anything, when I think of metre . . . It all depends on the *pause* – the natural pause, the natural *lingering* of the voice according to the feeling – it is the hidden *emotional* pattern that makes poetry, not the obvious form . . . It is the lapse of the feeling, something as indefinite as expression in the voice carrying emotion. It doesn't depend on the ear, particularly, but on the sensitive soul. And the ear gets a habit, and becomes master, when the ebbing and lifting emotion should be master, and the ear the transmitter . . . This is the constant war, I reckon, between new expression and the habituated, mechanical transmitters and receivers of the human constitution.

Whatever the general validity of these remarks (and we should remember the tendency of artists, already mentioned, to erect theories out of what they themselves do best), they certainly help to make clear not only how Lawrence thought about metre and rhyme ('use rhyme *accidentally*') they also help us to read his poems as they were meant to be read. Thus a finger-count would be of very little help in scanning the third stanza of 'Renascence' but if we trust 'the natural *lingering* of the voice according to the feeling' we shall find that the stresses come easily enough and pinpoint the key words:

> The little réd héifer: tonight I loóked in her éyes;
> She will cálve tomórrow.
> Lást níght, when I went with the lántern, the sów was grabbing her lítter
>
> With snárling réd jáws; and I heárd the críes
> Of the néw-bórn, and then the óld ówl, then the báts that flítter.

In a similar fashion, the shrinking in size of the last two stanzas corresponds to the narrowing of focus from the teeming life of nature to the perceiving self.

Thus, for all that it has a certain misty adolescent callowness about it ('Strange throbs, beyond laughter and tears') the poem is a quite considerable achievement for a youthful poet and clearly points the way he is to go.

Look! We Have Come Through!

In his Introduction to the *Collected Poems* (1928) Lawrence remarked with justice that some of his early poems were 'struggling to say something which it takes a man twenty years to be able to say'. He also felt that 'many of the poems are so personal that, in their fragmentary fashion, they make up a biography of an emotional and inner life'. Though he was referring specifically to the early poems of childhood and adolescent love, the words apply equally well to the sequence of poems, written between 1912 and 1917, which record the progress of the relationship between himself and the woman who had left husband and children to throw in her lot with him. Lawrence himself felt that his first departure from England with Frieda marked an important change in his life and under the pressure of the new experience he began to reach towards a new mode of poetic utterance. 'Even the best poetry, when it is at all personal', he wrote, 'needs the penumbra of its own time and place and circumstance to make it full and whole.' The sequence, which Lawrence called *Look! We Have Come Through!*, is an informal record of the day-to-day relationship between a man and his new bride from the early days of bliss through the times of strife and anxiety till they reach a mutually satisfactory awareness of themselves, and each other. In the words of the 'Argument' which Lawrence prefixed to the sequence:

> After much struggling and loss in love and in the world of man the protagonist throws in his lot with a woman who is already married. Together they go into another country, she perforce leaving her children behind. The conflict of love and hate goes on between the man and the woman, and between these two and the world around them till it reaches some sort of conclusion, they transcend into some condition of blessedness.

In his Foreword, Lawrence also warns against considering the individual poems as separate entities, insisting that they are 'intended as an essential story, or history, or confession, unfolding one from the other in organic development'. Reading the whole series through, we are likely to feel that the intention, however sincere, is not adequately realized in the achievement. Too often, the scenes of marital strife or harmony are imperfectly expressed in the slack rhythms and repetitions that do not accumulate into a lasting impression. We feel we are eavesdropping on the private quarrels of comparative strangers and may even sympathize with Bertrand Russell's waspish comment: 'They may have come through, but I don't see why *I* should look.' There are, roughly speaking, two sorts

Lawrence in 1920 when he first started growing his beard. Photo Bassano and Vandyke.

of poem in *Look! We Have Come Through!* Many poems are straight-forward attempts to depict psychological states or conflicts in the manner of which Lawrence the novelist was a master; the immediate model here was probably Meredith's *Modern Love*, though Lawrence is wholly without Meredith's glacial notion of poetic form. Inter-spersed with the psychological poems are a few lyrics celebrating the natural scene in which the lovers find themselves, some of them of a piercing clarity and delicacy. Of course the two kinds are not always separate and in a poem like 'Bei Hennef' we can see their not altogether successful union, but in general each kind is fairly easy to recognize. The 'psychological' poems are usually longer than the lyrics: one of the shorter and more successful among them is 'A Young Wife'.

A Young Wife

The pain of loving you
Is almost more than I can bear.

I walk in fear of you.
The darkness starts up where
You stand, and the night comes through
Your eyes when you look at me.

Ah never before did I see
The shadows that live in the sun!

Now every tall glad tree
Turns round its back to the sun
And looks down on the ground, to see
The shadow it used to shun.

At the foot of each glowing thing
A night lies looking up.

Oh, and I want to sing
And dance, but I can't lift up
My eyes from the shadows: dark
They lie spilt round the cup.

What is it? – Hark
The faint fine seethe in the air!

Like the seething sound in a shell!
It is death still seething where
The wild-flower shakes its bell
And the skylark twinkles blue –

> The pain of loving you
> Is almost more than I can bear.

The rhyme and metre here are more regular than is usual in these poems, but even here we can see that it is the 'hidden emotional pattern' that dictates the movement rather than 'footsteps hitting the earth'. Between the opening unrhymed couplet and its repetition at the close, a subtle psychological movement in the speaker is expressed powerfully if obliquely. What comes dangerously close to cliché at the opening is filled with substance at the end, so that we understand, or at least imaginatively realize what is involved in 'the pain of loving you'. We become aware that the fear of her husband which she confesses is not a matter of physical cowardice but a kind of dread of the man's otherness, the power of his separate existence:

> The darkness starts up where
> You stand,

And yet she realizes, in characteristically Lawrentian fashion, that the darkness is not merely negatively menacing but a source of power, the other side of the sun:

> Ah never before did I see
> The shadows that live in the sun!

A vague but powerful affinity is suggested between husband and wife on one hand and tree and shadow on the other, while the tree/shadow distinction also suggests the 'light' and 'dark' aspects of the man (and perhaps the woman). The movement changes from the anxiously reflective, through the exclamatory tone of the couplet just quoted to the exultant.

> Oh, and I want to sing
> And dance,

but this is quickly impeded by the rest of the stanza. The sense of new emotional life is strongly present in both the imagery and the tone of the six lines before the opening couplet is finally repeated. The whole poem, working by a unique mixture of direct statement and indirect image, is vividly evocative of the emotional turbulence within the young girl.

Among the lyrics, two of the finest are 'Green' and 'Gloire de Dijon'. The first has the visual concentration combined with emotional depth which the Imagist poets of the early twentieth century sought for. Lawrence himself had several poems published in the *Imagist Anthology*. 'Gloire de Dijon', a description of a woman taking a morning bath, is far more than mere description. It has the crystalline radiance of a Renoir painting.

When she rises in the morning
I linger to watch her;
She spreads the bath-cloth underneath the window
And the sunbeams catch her
Glistening white on the shoulders,
While down her sides the mellow
Golden shadow glows as
She stoops to the sponge, and her swung breasts
Sway like full-blown yellow
Gloire de Dijon roses.

She drips herself with water, and her shoulders
Glisten as silver, they crumple up
Like wet and falling roses, and I listen
For the sluicing of their rain-dishevelled petals.
In the window full of sunlight
Concentrates her golden shadow
Fold on fold, until it glows as
Mellow as the glory roses.

It also has the looser, more flexible rhythm that Lawrence was to use more and more frequently. Even the repetition of the flawed 'glows as/roses' rhyme does nothing to diminish the quality of rapt celebration that shines through this poem. It manages to combine rhymed and unrhymed lines of varying length in a way which expresses perfectly both the rhythm of the woman's leisurely movements as she pours water over herself and the surge of feeling within the man as he watches her.

Behind Lawrence's metrical experiments stand a variety of influences. The Authorized Version of the Bible and Whitman's *Leaves of Grass* are two of the earliest and most powerful, while later Lawrence consciously adopted and adapted some of the literary theories of the Italian Futurists, who declared among other things that

> Futurist free verse, a perpetual dynamism of thought, an uninterrupted stream of images and sounds, is the only medium to express the ephemeral, unstable and symphonic universe which is being created in us and with us.

This idea of a poetry whose form would capture the vivid reality of the moment as well as its fleeting insubstantiality found further expression in Lawrence's next important collection of poems.

Birds, Beasts and Flowers

From early childhood, long before he became a writer, Lawrence

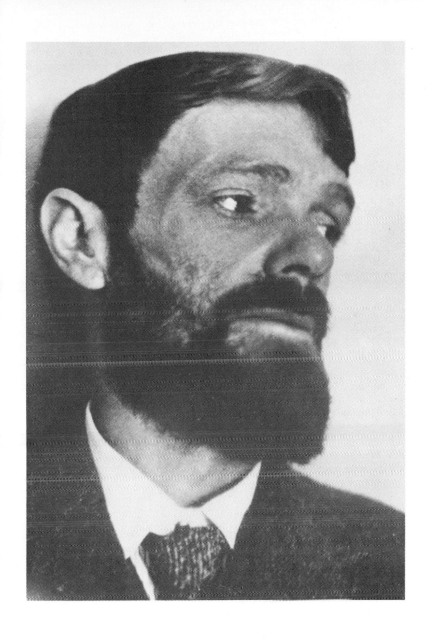

Lawrence c. 1924.

had an apprehension of the world about him that was far keener and more vivid than that of most people. As his creative vision developed, it embodied more and more the mature artist's sense of the vastness of life, its mystery and wonder, the otherness of various forms of existence and the necessity for human awareness to be in a right relationship with the rest of the life-process. These pre-occupations found powerful expression in the poems which make up the volume *Birds, Beasts and Flowers*, published in 1923 and consisting of poems written during his wanderings in Europe, Asia and the Americas. Lawrence is a Romantic poet in his reverence for the natural world, but he sees that world as far more restlessly active than most of the Romantics did. And he extends his sense of the non-human world to include the animal (including bird, fish and insect) kingdom which the Romantics virtually neglected. The freedom and flexibility of his verse grows as he gains in confidence and independence of vision, as these lines from 'Peach' illustrate:

> Why so velvety, why so voluptuous heavy,
> Why hanging with such inordinate weight?
> Why so indented?
>
> Why the groove?
> Why the lovely, bivalve roundnesses?
> Why the ripple down the sphere?
> Why the suggestion of incision?

The repetition and parallelism here remind us how much the young Lawrence was soaked in the Old Testament psalms whose structure depends on such patterns. Most of the best poems in *Birds, Beasts and Flowers* are too long to quote in full. Here is one that is not:

Humming Bird

I can imagine, in some otherworld
Primeval-dumb, far back
In that most awful stillness, that only gasped and hummed,
Humming-birds raced down the avenues.

Before anything had a soul,
While life was a heave of Matter, half inanimate,
This little bit chipped off in brilliance
And went whizzing through the slow, vast, succulent stems.

I believe there were no flowers then,
In the world where the humming-bird flashed ahead of creation.
I believe he pierced the slow vegetable veins with his long beak.

Probably he was big
As mosses, and little lizards, they say, were once big.

Probably he was a jabbing, terrifying monster.
We look at him through the wrong end of the long telescope of Time,
Luckily for us.

The very look of the poem on the page tells us at once that it conforms to no standard pattern of metre or rhyme. And as soon as we begin to read it aloud, we are carried along by its idiosyncratic but insistent rhythm, compounded of reflection, exploration and assertion, the voice of a man musing to himself and becoming intermittently conscious of a listener. The movement begins slowly and quietly and gathers speed in the third line, accelerating even further in 'Humming-birds raced down the avenues'. A similar contrast of tempo occurs between the first three lines and the last in the next verse, but in the final line of this stanza there is a sharp change of pace between 'And went whizzing through' and the near-solid obstacle presented by 'the slow, vast, succulent stems'.

The sense of a world newly created and only half-alive, with the tiny humming-bird as its growing point, is beautifully captured in the reference to 'the world where the humming-bird flashed ahead of creation' and the deliberate, purposive activity of the little creature is suggested by the heavy, insistent emphasis of the last line of the stanza.

The final stanza abruptly reverses the picture we have so far had, of the infinitesimal live creature pitted against the vast, dull vegetable growth which surrounds it. Now we are invited to see the humming-bird on a gigantic scale, an imaginative effort which recalls Blake's:

How do you know but every bird that cuts the airy way
Is an immense world of delight closed by your senses five?

Lawrence is not revealing a world of delight so much as an immense vista of unceasing life and growth. The poem ends almost light-heartedly, but underneath the banter is the disturbing vision of other worlds and other modes of being.

No selection, let alone a single poem, could adequately suggest the variety of tone, subject matter, metrical form and theme which is covered by the poems in *Birds, Beasts and Flowers*. They range from short lyrics like 'Peach' to long quasi-philosophical, reflective poems such as 'Fish', from humorously autobiographical encounters such as 'Mosquito' to the poignant evocations of sexuality in the 'Tortoise' poems. Together they form one of the most individual and exciting volumes of English poetry to appear in the first half of the twentieth century.

'Pansies' and 'Nettles'

Towards the end of his life, partly in response to the treatment he himself suffered as a writer and artist, partly as a result of growing bitterness at the way western civilisation seemed intent on committing spiritual suicide, Lawrence wrote a series of poems to which he himself gave the titles 'Pansies' and 'Nettles'. In his Introduction to the first collection of *Pansies* (1929) Lawrence neatly explains his title:

> This little bunch of fragments is offered as a bunch of *pensées*, anglicé pansies; a handful of thoughts. Or, if you will have the other derivation of pansy, from *panser*, to dress or soothe a wound; these are my tender administrations to the mental and emotional wounds we suffer from.

He goes on to explain that while each pansy has an intellectual aspect, it is not to be considered as an idea in isolation:

> Each little piece is a thought; not a bare idea, an opinion or a didactic statement, but a true thought, which comes as much from the heart and the genitals as from the head. A thought, with its own blood of emotion and instinct running in it like the fire in a fire-opal, if I may be so bold. Perhaps, if you hold up my pansies properly to the light, they may show a running vein of fire.

These remarks could apply to the best of Donne's poetry. It must be admitted that only a small number of Lawrence's poems fulfil the aspirations expressed here. Many of them are ill-tempered squibs, perfectly understandable given the provocation under which they were produced, but with little interest beyond their immediate occasion.

> Any woman who says to me
> – Do you really love me? –
> earns my undying detestation.

This is especially true of many pieces in the two posthumous collections, *More Pansies* (published in *Last Poems*, 1932) and *Nettles* (1930), which may be described as pansies with stings:

> O you hard-boiled conservatives, and you soft-boiled liberals
> don't you *see* how you make bolshevism inevitable?

It would require a light that never was on land or sea to show a running vein of fire in such effusions. On the other hand, there are a number of poems which do answer to Lawrence's description; one of the shortest and best of them is 'Desire is Dead':

> Desire may be dead
> and still a man can be
> a meeting place for sun and rain,
> wonder outwitting pain
> as in a wintry tree.

Lawrence seated under an olive tree near the Villa Mirenda, near Florence.

In a different, more epigrammatic mode Lawrence could be equally successful:

The Mosquito Knows

The mosquito knows full well, small as he is
he's a beast of prey.
But after all
he only takes his bellyful,
he doesn't put my blood in the bank.

Not all the poems in these collections are short lyrical or epigrammatic verses. 'Red Herring' and 'Nottingham's New University', for example, consist of several stanzas of satirical reflection on Lawrence's own Midland inheritance, the former more controlled and sustained than the latter.

One of the loveliest of the longer lyrics, and one which shows how subtly and delicately Lawrence handles his own free verse form, is 'Trees in the Garden'. This poem is deceptively simple. First of all it successfully captures the atmosphere of stillness before the storm, the feeling of hushed expectancy which we all become aware of. Secondly it gives us that sense of unearthliness which we are also sometimes conscious of when we look at a landscape when the air is heavy with approaching thunder. And lastly it presents the separate existence of the different trees, the movement of the lines almost conveying a sense of the different mode of being of each variety. 'The essential quality of poetry', Lawrence once wrote, 'is that it makes a new effort of attention, and "discovers" a new world within the known world.' 'Trees in the Garden' beautifully exemplifies what he meant.

Last Poems

From the time of his very first contact with it, the Mediterranean had exerted a powerful sway over Lawrence's imagination, and in the last few months of his life it inspired some of the loveliest poetry he wrote. At his death he was working on a long poem, 'The Ship of Death', which exists in several different versions, and it is possible that other poems which appear separately in *Last Poems* were intended to be part of this larger poem. Even in its unfinished form it is a magnificent poem, though too long to quote. The Mediterranean and the myths which belong to the people who lived round it were a source of perpetual inspiration to the dying poet, as the opening lines of 'Middle of the World' declare:

> This sea will never die, neither will it ever grow old
> nor cease to be blue, nor in the dawn
> cease to lift up its hills
> and let the slim black ship of Dionysos come smiling in
> with grape-vines up the mast, and dolphins leaping.

Figures such as Dionysos, Odysseus and Aphrodite haunt many of these last fine poems, though each of them acquires distinctively Lawrentian characteristics. Among the finest of these reworkings of classical myth is 'The Man of Tyre'. Here the poet visualises the rational, monotheistic Greek coming face to face with the rich actuality of sensual (sexual?) experience.

The central vision of the woman washing herself links this poem to one we have already met, 'Gloire de Dijon'. Here too the simple, everyday act is a celebration of the wonder and mystery of life in the flesh and the watching Greek, with his penchant for Platonic speculation, is compelled to utter a paean of praise. The sense of delight and extorted rapture is powerfully felt in the rhythm of the final stanza, while the series of 'who' clauses at the opening is a good example of Lawrence's ability to control the long variously stressed line which he used for most of his last poems. In contrast to the matter-of-fact directness of the two opening lines, the rest of the stanza has an incantatory rhythm which conveys the hypnotic spell which the sight of the woman bathing has on the man. In the middle section we ourselves feel the ecstatic vision of the beholder as the figure of the bathing woman is brought before us in all its naked actuality. Lines like

> with the full thighs slowly lifting of the wader wading shorewards
> and the shoulders pallid with light from the silent sky behind
> both breasts dim and mysterious, with the glamorous kindness of
>   twilight between them

do not merely paint a static picture but create a living figure in motion; only Lawrence could think of comparing 'the dim notch of black maidenhair' to 'an indicator' but the comparison is neither wanton nor weak. For it leads to the heart of the poem, the sense that the physical reality of life *is* the religious message that the woman has to give to the speculative Greek in all of us. God is both *in* life and is life itself. 'Man of Tyre' realizes this simple but profound insight not as an abstract idea but as felt experience.

Lawrence is a poet who, like most important poets, grows to greatness in our minds the longer and more deeply we read him. I hope the few poems discussed here will lead the reader to read more of the poetry. If he does, he will realize that, judged on his poetry alone, Lawrence is a creative writer of the very first rank.

9 Lawrence as literary critic

There is a kind of wry irony (which he probably would not have appreciated) in the fact that Lawrence who as a critic was *un*academic, in every possible sense of the word, should have been called 'the finest literary critic of our time – a great critic if ever there was one' by the outstanding academic literary critic of our time, F. R. Leavis. Though he did not write at length on Lawrence as a critic, Leavis was, as so often, the first to make a critical judgment whose validity is coming to be increasingly widely recognized.

It is not difficult to see the general affinity between Lawrence and Leavis as critics. A rigorous puritanism is one of the things they have in common. At its healthiest this is exemplified in Lawrence's dictum: 'The essential function of art is moral. Not aesthetic, not decorative, not pastime and recreation, but moral. ... ' Leavis' critical practice has also been in constant accordance with another celebrated pronouncement by Lawrence: 'Never trust the artist, trust the tale.' But for all that Lawrence is unlikely to have approved of the kind of criticism which Leavis and his followers have practised. For one thing, the close examination of literary texts and the relating of these to other relevant texts was not the way Lawrence usually went to work as a critic. For another, the implicit claim of objectivity which the Leavisians make, the assertion or assumption that they are appraising – 'evaluating' or 'revaluing' – a work of art which is indubitably *there* (one of the key words in the Leavisian critical vocabulary), is one which Lawrence had no patience with. Objectivity was a time-wasting will o'the wisp:

> All this critical twiddle-twaddle about style and form, all this pseudo-scientific classifying and analysing of books in an imitation-botanical fashion is mere impertinence and mostly dull jargon.
>
> 'John Galsworthy'

In that phrase 'mere impertinence' we hear the contempt of the practising craftsman for the interfering pedant. Lawrence would almost certainly have looked with disfavour on modern academic criticism, written as it is mostly by those who write nothing else. Finally, Lawrence had no use for 'tradition' either as Eliot or the academic critics understand it. That is to say, he did not have a consciousness of the whole of European literature from Homer to James Joyce in his bones, nor did he have the kind of systematic awareness of the literary past which would have enabled him to isolate George Eliot, Jane Austen, Joseph Conrad and Henry James as exemplars of The Great Tradition in the English Novel, or trace the 'line of wit' from Donne and Jonson through Marvell to Pope. But Lawrence is unlikely to have considered this a crippling inadequacy or an inadequacy at all. To him it would have been just as much 'pseudo-scientific classifying and analysing' and as such just as great an impertinence as the work of the Saintsburys and the Squires who were his immediate target. This brings us to the other notable similarity between Leavis and Lawrence – their supreme self-assurance, the intense conviction that what they are doing is all-important and, furthermore, that they are doing it better than anyone else.

The form and range of Lawrence's criticism

The only substantial critical work which Lawrence published in his lifetime was *Studies in Classic American Literature* which exists in different versions and which is a milestone in the serious study of early American writers such as Melville, Hawthorne, Cooper and Poe. The long *Study of Thomas Hardy*, which has already been discussed, was not published until after Lawrence's death. For the rest, his literary criticism found its way into reviews, occasional articles, prefaces, letters and even into the fiction. Taken together these form an impressive body of critical writing and one which spans his entire literary career.

Most of Lawrence's comments on particular writers relate to English, American and European literature of the nineteenth and twentieth centuries. He was also passionately interested, though in an informal way, in questions of literary theory and in problems connected with the relationship between art and morality.

Two things that strike the reader as soon as he begins reading any piece of criticism by Lawrence are informality and independence. The occasional nature of much of his criticism is matched by a flexible, improvised style which is much closer to speech than that of any other outstanding critic except Ezra Pound. Neither facile epigram nor mannered cadence nor parenthetical pedantry has any place in Lawrence's critical writing, though he sometimes falls victim to his own brand of jargon:

> The terrible fatality.
> Fatality.
> Doom.
> Doom! Doom! Doom! Something seems to whisper it in the very dark trees of America. Doom!
> Doom of what?
> Doom of our white day. We are doomed, doomed. And the doom is in America.
> The doom of our white day.

These spasms of apocalyptic apoplexy are fairly rare and even they are a sign that the writer is trying to convey not simply an abstract notion but the impact of a thought-sensation. We sense the fierce independence of the writer or perhaps we should say the speaker, for with Lawrence the critic as with Lawrence the novelist we are immediately and continuously aware of a speaking voice with an unmistakable rhythm, accent and vocabulary. On occasion he can be brilliantly witty but his aphorisms have a weight of seriousness behind them, a pressure of first-hand experience which makes them quite unlike the Wildean sort of epigram which dwindles into insignificance even as you savour it, like a chocolate drop melting in your mouth. Wit and seriousness are brought together in Lawrence in a way that after Lamb and Wilde seems impossible in prose: 'Sentimentalism is the working off on yourself of feelings you haven't really got.' 'Use rhyme *accidentally* – not as a sort of draper's rule for measuring lines off.' 'You may know a new utterance by the element of danger in it.' All of Lawrence's epigrams have the stamp of individuality about them; none of them are machine-turned.

Again, though nothing was more abhorrent to Lawrence than the artificial, brick-by-brick, burn-with-a-hard-gemlike-flame prose of the professional essayists, his critical prose has a distinctive rhythm of its own which often manages to combine the vitality of speech with the dignity of a more formal mode of utterance. Here too the source of Lawrence's strength is his absolute integrity, the passionate commitment which Pound was talking about when he said a man should stake everything on a single judgment:

> Thomas Mann seems to me the last sick sufferer from the complaint of Flaubert. The latter stood away from life as from a leprosy . . . Already I find Thomas Mann, who as he says, fights so hard against the banal in his work, somewhat banal. His expression may be very fine. But by now what he expresses is stale. I think we have learned our lesson, to be sufficiently aware of the fulsomeness of life. And even while he has a rhythm in style, yet his work has none of the rhythm of a living thing . . . Even *Madame Bovary* seems to me dead in respect of the living rhythm of the whole work. While it is there in *Macbeth* like life itself.

'Thomas Mann', 1912

The background of reading which Lawrence brought to his criticism has already been briefly noted. Without being in the slightest degree pedantic, he was able to make use of an enormous if slightly eccentric range of books in a wholly individual way, as for instance in his conjectures on the historical relation between syphilis and figure painting in *Introduction to these Paintings*.

Critical theory and pratice

A good way to approach Lawrence's literary criticism is through the opening of the famous essay on Galsworthy from which I have already quoted. 'Literary criticism,' Lawrence writes, ' can be no more than a *reasoned* account of the feeling produced upon the critic by the book he is criticising.' And immediately afterwards he adds: 'The touchstone is emotion, *not reason*. We judge a work of art by its effect on our sincere and vital emotion *and by nothing else*.' (My italics.) This disjunction between emotion and reason, combined with an uncomfortable awareness that reason must be given its due (that Lawrence was a very intelligent man in the ordinary meaning of the word hardly needs insisting on) bedevils much of Lawrence's criticism while giving it its unique flavour. Reading him we often feel that we are watching an expert rider changing horses in midstream, or perhaps riding both horses at once. Thus in the same essay it is possible to find a sober, straightforward, closely reasoned piece of writing –

> In his 'human' self Melville is almost dead. That is, he hardly reacts to human contacts any more; or only ideally: or just for a moment. His human-emotional self is almost played out. He is abstract, self analytical and abstracted. And he is more spellbound by the strange slidings and collidings of Matter than by the things men do. In this he is like Dana. It is the material elements he really has to do with. His drama is with them. He was a futurist long before futurism found paint. The sheer naked slidings of the elements. And the human soul experiencing it all. So often, it is almost over the border: psychiatry. Almost spurious. Yet so great.

> 'Herman Melville's *Moby Dick*'

– and passages of dithyrambic doom-doom-dooming like the one already quoted. Yet when he was guided by his best insights, Lawrence's criticism was pertinent and often profound. He recognized implicitly that every piece of criticism was inevitably an attempt to make the best of two half-truths – that of the complete objectivity of the work of art and that of the complete autonomy of the critic's feelings about it. In the essay on Galsworthy he writes: 'A critic must be able to feel the impact of a work of art in all its complexity and force.' But this is by no means as easy as it may appear, for it is a matter that goes beyond and below conscious decision. 'To do this', Lawrence continues,

> he must be a man of force and complexity himself, which very few critics are. A man with a paltry, impudent nature will never write anything but paltry, impudent criticism ... The more scholastically educated a man is generally, the more he is an emotional boor.

But not only must the good critic be 'emotionally alive in every fibre', he must also be 'intellectually capable and skilful in essential logic'. The insistence on intellectual capacity and logical skill ('essential logic' I take to mean the kind of sympathetic reasoning relevant to the drawing out of the inner form of a given work) completes the equation beginning with 'A critic must be able to *feel* the impact of a work of art . . . ' (my italics). In addition

> a good critic should give his reader a few standards to go by. He can change the standards for every new critical attempt, so long as he keeps good faith. But it is just as well to say: This and this is the standard we judge by.

It will be clear that impersonality and obliteration of the self in the manner advocated by Eliot and Joyce was not for Lawrence a desirable goal for either artist or critic. Indeed, in certain circumstances it could be a kind of cheating, an evasion of the real encounter between the artist and his experience or the critic and the work. But there *is* a kind of ideal of the impersonal work of art lurking within Lawrence's theory of fiction too. Though, as we have seen, he valued art because it was essentially moral in its function, its morality was entirely dependent on its being art in the first place. And the true morality of the work of art lay in the degree to which it quickened the perceiver's awareness of the difference between the conscious moral code of the artist and the essential morality of the work itself, which would always be in conflict with the former. This is how he puts the matter in Chapter IX of the *Study of Thomas Hardy*:

> For the moralist it is easy. He can insist on that aspect of the Law or Love which is in the immediate line of development for his age, and he can sternly or severely exclude or suppress all the rest.
>
> So that all morality is of temporary value, useful to its times. But Art must give a deeper satisfaction. It must give fair play all round.
>
> Yet every work of art adheres to some system of morality. *But if it be really a work of art, it must contain the essential criticism on the morality to which it adheres . . .*
>
> The degree to which the system of morality, or the metaphysic, of any work of art is submitted to criticism within the work of art makes the lasting value and satisfaction of that work. (My italics.)

These comments should be seen as an explication of the caution 'Never trust the artist, trust the tale.' They also lie behind Lawrence's remark in the first chapter of *Studies in Classic American Literature* that 'Art-speech is the only truth.' And they explain just why Lawrence set so much store by the novel as 'the one bright book of life'. Because he believed that life consisted 'not in facts but a flow', the novel seemed to him the form most finely adapted to convey the very pulse of this flow to our sympathetic consciousness – to 'lead it into new places' or 'away . . . from things gone dead' (*Lady Chatterley's Lover*, Chapter IX).

Thus the morality which the true novel is concerned with is not a formalized ethical code but 'that delicate, for ever trembling and changing *balance* between me and my circumambient universe which precedes and accompanies a true relatedness'. This is why Lawrence declared

> . . . I am a novelist. And being a novelist, I consider myself superior to the saint, the scientist, the philosopher, and the poet, who are all great masters of different bits of man alive, but never get the whole hog.
>
> 'Why the Novel Matters'.

The chief virtue of the novel is that by its very commitment to the flow of experience it resists any attempt to formulate and fix the quick of life in a static code of convention:

> Philosophy, religion, science, they are all of them busy nailing things down, to get a stable equilibrium . . .
>
> But the novel, no. The novel is the highest example of subtle inter-relatedness that man has discovered. Everything is true in its own time, place, circumstance, and untrue outside of its own place, time, circumstance. If you try to nail anything down in the novel, either it kills the novel, or the novel gets up and walks away with the nail.
>
> 'Morality and the Novel'.

These observations are at least as applicable to Lawrence's own novels as to those of any other writer. *The Plumed Serpent* and *Lady Chatterley's Lover*, for instance, strike me as novels which have been killed, or at least grievously wounded by the attempt to nail something down in them, while *Women in Love* is a triumphant example of a novel which gets up and walks away with the nail.

Lawrence was the most personal of critics. 'If an author arouses my deeper sympathy,' he wrote reviewing William Carlos Williams' *In the American Grain*, 'he can have as many faults as he likes'. Conversely when that sympathy was not aroused he could be very severe, as in his judgment on H. G. Wells' *The World of William Clissold*:

> This work is not a novel because it contains none of the passional and emotional reactions which are at the root of all thought and which must be conveyed in a novel. This book is all chewed-up newspaper and chewed-up scientific reports, like a mouse's nest.

All facts and no flow, in other words. It is clear that a great deal of Lawrence's critical writing even when, perhaps especially when, it pretends to be objective falls into the category of How I Work. That is to say he uses the works of other writers to illustrate ideas or problems that interest him as a novelist. He himself was of course perfectly well aware of this, as he showed when he remarked that his study of Thomas Hardy would be about anything but Hardy. Reading the twenty-five-odd pages on *Jude the Obscure* we are more aware of the novel Lawrence might have written than the one that Hardy actually wrote, but we also see Hardy from a fascinating, highly personal yet not wholly arbitrary standpoint. It is no accident that Lawrence devoted his most sustained critical attention to those writers whom he felt to have been pioneers in territory he himself was drawn to explore further. For instance, his reading of *Moby Dick* – 'mind-consciousness extinguishes blood-consciousness and consumes the blood' – makes sense mainly in the light of Lawrence's own achievement in fiction. But it does show us a side of Melville's masterpiece that no one had hitherto seen and one which has been found persuasive or stimulating or both ever since. Similarly his essay on Whitman is a masterpiece of sympathetic demolition showing as much insight into the critic's own weaknesses as into his subject's.

In view of the widespread but wholly mistaken belief that Lawrence took himself and his ideas with unremitting seriousness, not to say solemnity, and was incapable of self-criticism, it needs to be reaffirmed that he was one of the best critics of his own work. Since examples of this have already been offered in other contexts I shall cite only one more, probably the most often quoted of Lawrence's judgments on his own work. It occurs in a letter to Edward Garnett in which Lawrence is defending himself against the charge that he is not sufficiently interested in individual character. The novel in question is a version of *The Rainbow*:

> You mustn't look in my novel for the old stable *ego* of the character. There is another *ego*, according to whose action the individual is unrecognisable, and passes through, as it were, allotropic states which it needs a deeper sense than any we've been used to exercise, to discover are states of the same single radically unchanged element.

The implications of these remarks have been discussed elsewhere in this book; here they are quoted to illustrate Lawrence's unerring sense of exactly what he was trying to do and how he was doing it.

Literature and life

As a critic Lawrence was constantly reaching out from the given work to its implications for living and for human relationships. Sometimes he showed an unseemly haste in rushing from the work to the world, and his impatience with formal problems in the narrow sense of the word is often evident. 'Every work of art has its own form, which has no relation to any other form', he asserts, which is partly true but unhelpful. Even more forthrightly he declares: 'They want me to have form. That means they want me to have *their* pernicious, ossiferous skin-and-grief form; and I won't.' His achievement proves that he was quite justified in his view as far as his own work was concerned and his obliviousness to form in the external sense did not prevent him from making subtle and sensitive judgments on particular works. But a feature of Lawrence's criticism as unmistakable as his independence is the insistence that literature matters because it can shape our lives in ways that go far below the alteration of codes of conduct. This conviction often makes his criticism fiercely partisan – 'Art for my sake' and 'Before everything I like sincerity and a quickening spontaneous rhythm' are typically Lawrentian declarations – but it is just this passionate partiality which makes his criticism exciting to read. Lawrence has nearly all the qualities one looks for in a critic: independence of outlook and freshness of approach, the creative artist's awareness of and interest in practical problems, a catholic background, sympathy and understanding (intense within a limited sphere), high intelligence and wide-ranging knowledge, an energetic curiosity about the rationale of both criticism and creative writing and a gift for utterance that is as memorable as it is distinctive. And, perhaps surprisingly, he even has his own kind of humility, both genuine and appropriate. After some sharply critical remarks on H. G. Wells, he writes, 'I do like him and esteem him and wish I knew half as much about things.' Lawrence both recognized and avoided the temptation of the critic to speak from lofty heights:

> It would be easy enough to rise in critical superiority as a critic always feels he must, superior to his author, and find fault ... heaven save me from feeling superior just because I have a chance to snarl. I am only too thankful that Mr Williams wrote his book.

Review of *In the American Grain*.

There speaks the critic who is also fully in sympathy with the creative artist because he is one himself.

10 Lawrence's plays

There is no space here for more than a brief general account of Lawrence's career as a playwright. During his lifetime, two of his plays were performed and these as well as one other were published at first separately, then in a single volume. *The Widowing of Mrs Holroyd*, perhaps his best play, based on the same material as his short story 'The Odour of Chrysanthemums', was published in 1914, though Lawrence showed a version of it to Jessie Chambers when she visited him in Croydon. The play had an amateur production at Altrincham, Cheshire in 1920 and a professional one by the London Stage Society under the direction of Esmé Percy in 1926. One of the members of the audience at the latter was Bernard Shaw, who later remarked that in comparison with Lawrence's, his own dialogue was stiff and artificial. When the play was successfully revived at the Royal Court Theatre, London in 1968, the critic Ronald Bryden described Lawrence as

> a master of concentration, of burning intensity, distilling from a naturalism homely as potatoes a fiery, white and ice-cold emotion which shocks like a gulp of liquid energy ... When she [Mrs Holroyd] bends over her husband's body to wash it, the whole movement and cumulative meaning of the play gathers in her gesture like a breaking wave.

The only other Lawrence play to be performed in his lifetime was also put on by the Stage Society in 1927 but is in a very different manner. *David* is a fairly close adaptation of the Old Testament story, focusing on the tension between Saul and David. David can destroy Saul, but cannot himself amount to anything. As Jonathan says to him:

> I would not see thy new day, David. For thy wisdom is the wisdom of the subtle, and behind thy passion lies prudence. And naked thou wilt not go into the fire.

Lawrence is generally successful in his use of a quasi-Biblical language in this play, but the failure of the stage production disheartened him and he made no more real efforts to have his plays staged.

His first play, *A Collier's Friday Night*, with its ironic reference to the title of Burns' poem, was written as early as 1906. It is a vivid and powerful portrayal of working class life seen wholly from within, with the economic, social and emotional pressures of domestic life conveyed in dialogue of unforgettable immediacy. It is clear proof that given a more sympathetic reception in the professional theatre,

Lawrence could have been one of the great English dramatists of the century.

Touch and Go (published in 1920) was written a few years earlier and was to be part of a project initiated by Douglas Goldring, 'Plays for a People's Theatre'. In his Preface to the play, Lawrence asserted that the essential requirements of a people's theatre were cheap seats and plays that were really about people:

> Not mannequins. Not lords nor proletarians nor bishops nor husbands nor co-respondents nor virgins nor adulteresses nor uncles nor noses. Not even white rabbits nor presidents. People. Men who are somebody, not men who are something.

But the play itself hardly lives up to these large aspirations. The central situation of the conflict between the mine owner and his men is rather sentimentally evaded in the peace-maker's sincere but inane appeal, apparently endorsed by the dramatist to 'leave off struggling against one another, and set up a new state of things'.

Three less ambitious plays, all dating from the years 1910 to 1912, are *Fight for Barbara*, first published in 1933 as *Keeping Barbara*, a largely autobiographical account of the tension in Frieda between her children and Lawrence, *The Married Man*, a feeble play based on the misadventures of a womanizing friend of Lawrence's youth, and *The Merry-Go-Round*, a mildly amusing domestic comedy of Eastwood life which has been successfully revived on the professional stage. But, with the possible exception of *Mrs Holroyd*, Lawrence's finest play is *The Daughter-in-Law* which was also memorably revived at the Royal Court in 1968. Here Lawrence returns once again to working class life as he had known it, and to a theme with which he was agonizingly familiar. The play centres on the efforts of Minnie Gascoigne to restore her husband to the manhood and independence which has been systematically drained out of him by the possessive love of his mother. Once again, the force and intensity of Lawrence's dialogue are quite unique in English drama of the time, or indeed of any time since.

As in most other areas of his creative activity, Lawrence was ahead of his age in drama. It is only in the recent past that most of his plays have triumphantly vindicated themselves on the stage. The plays have been published in a single volume as *The Complete Plays of D. H. Lawrence* (1965).

Part Three
Reference section

Short biographies

ALDINGTON, RICHARD, 1892–1962. Novelist, poet and critic, Aldington first met Lawrence on the eve of the First World War and they met again in 1926 and 1928, when the Lawrences were his guests at Ile de Port-Cros. Aldington edited Lawrence's *Last Poems* (1932) and an anthology of Lawrence's writings *The Spirit of Place* and wrote *D. H. Lawrence: Portrait of a Genius But . . .* (1950).

BENNETT, ARNOLD, 1868–1931. A novelist who was one of the leading figures on the English literary scene in the early twentieth century. Lawrence was very critical of Bennett as a novelist, calling him 'an old imitator' but had reason to be grateful for Bennett's generosity and personal kindness which he acknowledged. For his part Bennett was convinced of Lawrence's genius, though he had reservations about his literary craftsmanship.

BRETT, THE HON. DOROTHY E., 1891–1979. A British-born painter, daughter of Viscount Esher, who lived most of her life in Taos, where she first went to join the Lawrences in 1924. She painted many pictures of Lawrence and wrote an autobiography, *Lawrence and Brett* (1933), in which she refers to herself throughout as 'Brett', the name she liked to be addressed by.

BREWSTER, EARL AND ACHSAH. Lawrence's American friends, painters and students of Oriental philosophy, they persuaded Lawrence to follow them to Ceylon and remained his friends to the end of his life. Their account of Lawrence, *D. H. Lawrence: Reminiscences and Correspondence*, appeared in 1934.

BURROWS, LOUISE ('LOUIE'), 1888–1962. A girl whom Lawrence met while they were both pupil-teachers at Ilkeston (1903–5) and to whom Lawrence proposed marriage in 1910. Their relationship came to an end in 1912, but many years later she visited Lawrence's grave at Vence.

CARSWELL, CATHERINE, 1879–1946. Scottish writer, a staunch supporter of Lawrence from the first. Her sympathetic review of *The Rainbow* resulted in her being dropped as a contributor to the *Glasgow Herald* after ten years. She wrote an account of Lawrence entitled *The Savage Pilgrimage* (1932, 1951).

CHAMBERS, ALAN, 1882–1946. Eldest brother of Jessie Chambers and a model for George Saxton in *The White Peacock*. He married Lawrence's first cousin Alvina and emigrated to Canada.

CHAMBERS, JESSIE, 1887–1944. The 'Miriam' of *Sons and Lovers* and Lawrence's youthful love. She was, according to Lawrence himself, responsible for launching him on his literary career and has written a memorable record of their relationship, under the initials E.T., entitled *D. H. Lawrence: A Personal Record* (1935).

CLARKE, ADA, 1887–1948. Lawrence's younger sister. Co-author with G. Stuart Gelder of *Young Lorenzo: Early Life of D. H. Lawrence* (1932).

CORKE, HELEN, 1882–1978. A Croydon schoolteacher who met Lawrence while he was at the Davidson Road School. Lawrence's second novel, *The Trespasser*, was based on her diary and other papers. Her own fictional version of this real-life episode appeared as *Neutral Ground* in 1933. Lawrence proposed to her and was rejected. She wrote *Lawrence and Apocalypse* (1933) and *D. H. Lawrence's 'Princess'* (1951), the latter an account of Jessie Chambers of whom she was a close friend.

DOUGLAS, NORMAN, 1868–1952. Writer and bon viveur who first met Lawrence in 1909 and again during the latter's stay in Florence. Introduced Lawrence to Maurice Magnus and defended him against Lawrence in a pamphlet. Was the model for James Argyle in *Aaron's Rod*.

GARNETT, EDWARD, 1868–1937. Critic, essayist and publisher's editor, Edward Garnett came from a famous literary family. His father was the Victorian writer Richard Garnett and his wife, Constance, translated many Russian authors into English. He met Lawrence through Ford Madox Ford and was a firm but very sympathetic critic. He also helped the Lawrences during the early days of their marriage. The manuscript of *Sons and Lovers* with Garnett's revisions shows what a discerning and sensitive editor he was. His son David Garnett wrote of Lawrence in a volume of autobiography *The Golden Echo* (1953).

HESELTINE, PHILIP, 1894–1930. An English composer who adopted the pseudonym of Peter Warlock. A neighbour of the Lawrences in Cornwall, Heseltine later broke with Lawrence and threatened to sue him over the latter's representation of him as Halliday in *Women in Love*.

HOPKIN, WILLIAM E. 1862–1951. Journalist and Eastwood local councillor and a devoted friend of Lawrence throughout his life. He made a valuable collection of material relating to Lawrence, now in the Eastwood Public Library, and through him Lawrence came into contact with some of the leading socialists and freethinkers of the day.

Edward Garnett with his son David, the novelist.

HUEFFER, FORD MADOX, 1873–1939. Grandson of the Victorian painter Ford Madox Brown, Hueffer changed his surname to Ford at the outbreak of the First World War. He founded *The English Review* in 1908 and the following year gave Lawrence his first London appearance in print. In addition to the sequence of novels entitled *Parade's End*, Hueffer also wrote a volume of autobiography, *Return to Yesterday* (1931), in which he gives a highly coloured account of a visit to Lawrence.

HUXLEY, ALDOUS, 1894–1963. Novelist, essayist, poet, Huxley met Lawrence in 1915 and immediately came under his spell. From 1926 he was often with the Lawrences and he was at his bedside when Lawrence died. He edited Lawrence's *Letters* (1932), for which he wrote a superb introduction. Lawrence appears as Rampion in Huxley's novel *Point Counterpoint*. ('Your Rampion is a gas-bag', Lawrence wrote.)

KING, EMILY, 1882–1962. Lawrence's older sister.

KOTELIANSKY, SAMUEL SOLOMNOVICH ('KOT') 1882–1955. Born in the Ukraine, Koteliansky came to England just before the beginning of the First World War on a scholarship from the University of Kiev for research in economics. He became well known as a translator from the Russian, collaborating with Lawrence. Katherine Mansfield, Leonard and Virginia Woolf and others in translating Tolstoy, Dostoevsky, Chekhov and several other writers. He remained one of Lawrence's staunchest friends.

LAWRENCE, ARTHUR JOHN, 1846–1924. Lawrence's father, a miner at Brinsley Colliery, Long remembered locally for his good fellowship and dancing skill. He first met Lawrence's mother at a party given by a mutual relative.

LAWRENCE, FRIEDA, 1879–1956. Second daughter of Baron and Baroness Friedrich von Richthofen and a distant cousin of the legendary First World War German air ace nicknamed The Red Baron, Frieda married Ernest Weekley in 1899 and had three children. The marriage was dissolved in May 1914 and in July (1934). In 1950 she married Angelino Ravagli who looked after the Lawrence property in New Mexico.
Frieda married Lawrence. She was an active collaborator in much of Lawrence's writing and wrote her own account of her years with Lawrence in a fascinating autobiography, *Not I, But the Wind*

LAWRENCE, LYDIA (née BEARDSALL), 1852–1910. Lawrence's mother, a former schoolmistress and a profound influence on the novelist. The values of respectability, gentility, worldly success and intellectual distinction which she represented for him were increasingly subjected to criticism both in his novels and discursive writings. Her early influence undoubtedly led to the break-up of Lawrence's relationship with Jessie Chambers. Her death by cancer is the subject of many poems as well as a central episode in *Sons and Lovers*.

LAWRENCE, WILLIAM ERNEST, 1878–1901. Lawrence's elder brother and the apple of his mother's eye till his tragic death, described in *Sons and Lovers*.

MAGNUS, MAURICE, 1876–1920. Once Isadora Duncan's manager, later a member of the Foreign Legion, Magnus was introduced to Lawrence by Norman Douglas. Lawrence wrote the Introduction to his *Memoirs of the Foreign Legion*. Magnus committed suicide in Malta.

MANSFIELD, KATHERINE, 1888–1923. Katherine Mansfield was born Katherine Beauchamp in Wellington, New Zealand and achieved fame as a short story writer. In 1918 she divorced her first husband and married John Middleton Murry with whom she had been living for some time. The Murrays were witnesses at the Lawrences' wedding and neighbours of the Lawrences during part of the war, first at Chesham, Bucks, and later in Cornwall. Katherine Mansfield died of tuberculosis in southern France.

MARSH, SIR EDWARD, 1872–1953. Editor of *Georgian Poetry* (1912–1922) which published some of Lawrence's poems. He met the Lawrences in Kent in 1913 and remained a good and generous friend. Lawrence's letters to him contain some excellent comments on poetry and on particular Georgian poets such as W. H. Davies.

MERRILD, KNUD, 1895 1954. Danish painter who, with his friend Kai Götszche, was a neighbour of the Lawrences at the Del Monte Ranch in Taos and later met Lawrence in Los Angeles. His narrative of the Lawrences, *A Poet and Two Painters*, appeared in 1939.

MORRELL, LADY OTTOLINE, 1873–1938. A famous literary hostess whose country home, Garsington Manor in Oxfordshire, was the meeting place for many of the leading literary and artistic figures of the day. She met Lawrence in 1915 and was a devoted admirer till she learned of his portrayal of her as Hermione Roddice in *Women in Love*.

MURRY, JOHN MIDDLETON, 1889–1957. Murry first met Lawrence in 1913 and became a devoted, perhaps too devoted, disciple, leading to the inevitable rejection by Lawrence. He was editor of *The Athenaeum* (1919–21) and *The Adelphi* (1923–30) as well as author of several books of criticism and biography including two on

Lawrence, *Son of Woman* (1931, 1954) and *Reminiscences of D. H. Lawrence* (1933).

RUSSELL, BERTRAND, 3rd EARL RUSSELL, 1872–1970. Mathematician, philosopher and political campaigner, Russell first met Lawrence through Lady Ottoline Morrell in 1915. Through him Lawrence visited Cambridge, which he loathed. Russell and Lawrence planned a series of lectures against war but nothing came of the project and their fundamental antipathy of outlook and temperament soon led to the end of their friendship. Russell appears as Sir Josiah Mattheson in *Women in Love*. In his autobiography, Russell says he did not realize at the time of their association that Lawrence's views led straight to the German concentration camps of the Second World War.

TROTTER, DOROTHY (née WARREN), 1896–1954. Niece of Lady Ottoline Morrell and owner of the Warren Gallery, Maddox Street, London where Lawrence's ill-fated exhibition of paintings was held in 1929. She met Lawrence at Garsington and Hampstead in 1915.

WEEKLEY, ERNEST, 1865–1954. Ernest Weekley, Frieda's first husband, was a distinguished etymologist and Head of the Department of Modern Languages at Nottingham University College when Lawrence was a student there. It was while on a visit to Weekley's home in Mapperley to discuss the possibility of a job in a German university that Lawrence first met Frieda.

Sketch map showing some of the places associated with Lawrence's childhood and youth.

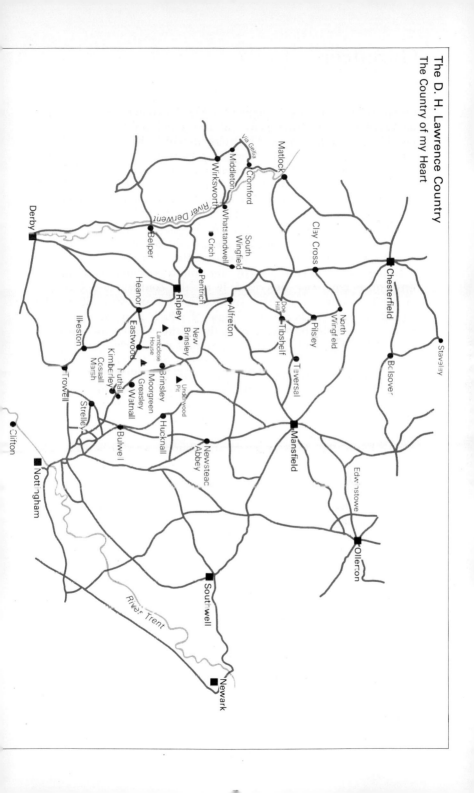

The D. H. Lawrence Country
The Country of my Heart

Gazetteer

EASTWOOD is somewhat changed since Lawrence's day and the advent of pit-head baths means that the visitor is unlikely to see black-faced miners in the streets. The house in which the writer was born, now 8a Victoria Street, is carefully preserved as a typical miner's dwelling of the period and is open to visitors. His other childhood home in The Breach, now Garden Road, is also open as a D. H Lawrence museum and the local library has a Hopkin-Lawrence Room with a good collection of material relating to Lawrence. Other places associated with Lawrence still standing in Eastwood include the Albert Street Congregational Chapel, the Beauvale Board School and the Rising Sun, one of Lawrence senior's haunts.

Despite the motorway nearby, the countryside has changed very little since Lawrence described it as 'the country of my heart'. Haggs Farm and Felley Mill are derelict, but one can still see the view from the Walker Street house of which Lawrence wrote 'I know that view better than any in the world.' Not far away are the ruins of Beauvale Abbey, the background for the early short story 'A Fragment of Stained Glass'. Just north of Eastwood is Moorgreen Reservoir, the Nethermere of *The White Peacock* and the Willey Water of *Women in Love*. Lamb Close, the home of the mine-owning Barbers which appears under different names in *The White Peacock*, *Women in Love* and *Lady Chatterley's Lover*, is nearby. Due south lies the village of Cossall, the Cossethay of *The Rainbow* where the original Marsh Farm, the church cottage and church can still be seen. The visitor who is new to it may be surprised by the lushness of much of the Midland landscape around the Misk Hills which Lawrence described as 'an extremely beautiful countryside, just between the red sandstone and the oak-trees of Nottingham and the cold limestone, the ash-trees, the stone fences of Derbyshire'.

In NOTTINGHAM itself, the High School to which Lawrence won a scholarship and University College which he attended from 1906 to 1908 are still there, the latter building now housing the Public Library. In the Castle may be seen some of the pictures which fired the young Lawrence's imagination.

The map shows Lawrence's continental journeys, and, though exposed to tourism on a scale never imagined by Lawrence, many places on the route are still much as he described them in, among other books, *Twilight in Italy* (1916).

The War Years: Berkshire, Sussex, Oxfordshire, Cornwall

CHESHAM, Bucks: The cottage at which Lawrence spent the first few

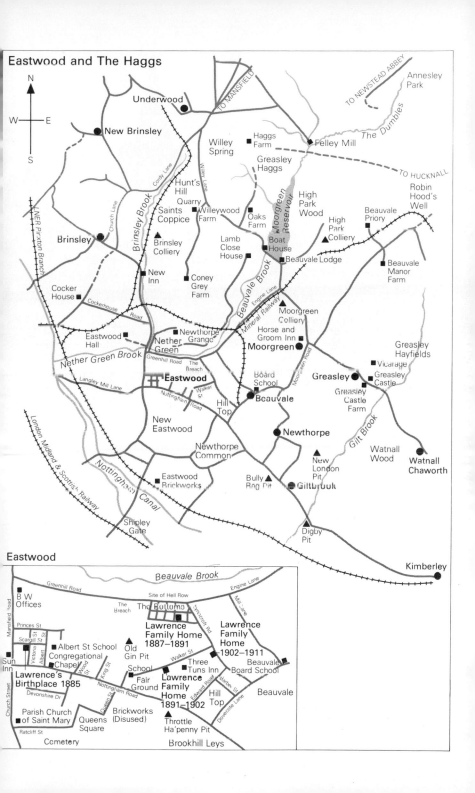

Eastwood and The Haggs

N
W — E
S

TO MANSFIELD

TO NEWSTEAD ABBEY

Annesley Park

Underwood

New Brinsley

Willey Spring

Haggs Farm

Greasley Haggs

Felley Mill

The Dumbles

TO HUCKNALL

Hunt's Hill Quarry

Saints Coppice

Willeywood Farm

Oaks Farm

Moorgreen Reservoir

High Park Wood

Robin Hood's Well

Brinsley

Brinsley Colliery

Lamb Close House

Beauvale Priory

High Park Colliery

Brinsley Brook

Corby Lane

Church Lane

Willey Lane

LNER Pinxton Branch

New Inn

Coney Grey Farm

Boat House

Beauvale Lodge

Beauvale Manor Farm

Cocker House

Cockerhouse Road

Eastwood Hall

Newthorpe Grange

Nether Green

Beauvale Brook

Engine Lane

Mineral Railway

Horse and Groom Inn

Moorgreen Colliery

Moorgreen

Greasley Hayfields

Nether Green Brook

Greenhill Road

The Breach

Eastwood

Board School

Beauvale

Moorgreen Road

Vicarage

Greasley

Greasley Castle

Greasley Castle Farm

Langley Mill Lane

Nottingham Road

Walker St

Hill Top

London Midland & Scottish Railway

New Eastwood

Newthorpe Common

Newthorpe

Gilt Brook

Watnall Wood

Watnall Chaworth

Nottingham Canal

Eastwood Brickworks

Bully Bog Pit

New London Pit

Giltbrook

Shipley Gate

Digby Pit

Kimberley

Eastwood

Beauvale Brook

Greenhill Road

Engine Lane

B W Offices

Site of Hell Row

The Breach

The Bottoms

Mansfield Road

Princes St

Scargill St

Albert St School

Congregational Chapel

Old Gin Pit

Synderhill Rd

Mill Lane

Lawrence Family Home 1887–1891

Lawrence Family Home 1902–1911

Sun Inn

Victoria St

Albert St

Wood St

King St

School

Three Tuns Inn

Walker St

Beauvale Board School

Lawrence's Birthplace 1885

Nottingham Road

Devonshire Dr

Fair Ground

Lawrence Family Home 1891–1902

Queens Square

Hill Top

Edward Road

Birdro St

Dovecote Lane

Beauvale

Church Street

Parish Church of Saint Mary

Brickworks (Disused)

Throttle Ha'penny Pit

Ratcliff St

Cemetery

Brookhill Leys

Cossall Church, the Cossethay of The Rainbow.

months of the war and grew the beard he wore for the rest of his life is here. He wrote some of the *Prussian Officer* stories here.

GREATHAM, Pulborough, Sussex: The Catholic writers Wilfrid and Alice Meynell had bought for their daughters a small circle of old cottages. Viola Meynell, their daughter, offered her own, Shed Hall, to the Lawrences who lived there from January to July 1915. Here Lawrence wrote 'England, My England' with a central character based on the husband of one of the Meynell girls. He also completed *The Rainbow* at Greatham.

GARSINGTON MANOR, Oxon: This is the origiginal of Breadalby in *Women in Love*, the home of a famous Georgian hostess, Lady Ottoline Morrell, where Lawrence, who was a frequent visitor throughout 1915, met such figures as Bertrand Russell and Aldous Huxley.

HIGHER TREGERTHEN, near Zennor, Cornwall: The little two-roomed stone cottage where the Lawrences spent nearly two years of the war and where the Murrys visited them is in this village. Among other things he worked on *Women in Love* here.

CEYLON AND AUSTRALIA: 'Ardanaree', the house in Kandy where Lawrence lived for three weeks, is still standing, though the view Lawrence had from it is obscured. Kandy itself is virtually unchanged since Lawrence's time, though like most other places it is more crowded.

'Wyewurk' in Thirroul, Western Australia, is the cottage looking out on to the Pacific ocean where Lawrence wrote *Kangaroo*.

NEW MEXICO AND MEXICO. Kiowa Ranch in Taos, New Mexico has become something of a holy of holies for Lawrence lovers. Here may be seen Lawrence's (and Frieda's) tomb, in a building originally surmounted by a phoenix, inadvertently replaced with an eagle by Angelino Ravagli. In Taos Lawrence competes for the visitor's attention with another eminent figure associated with the area who also has a museum devoted to him. This is Kit Carson, the Wild West pioneer.

The surrounding countryside seems to be much as it was fifty years ago. It inspired much of Lawrence's writings, including the fine novella 'St Mawr'. Southwards across the border in Chapala, Mexico is the house by the lake where the Lawrences lived for a time. This is the setting of part of *The Plumed Serpent* and *Mornings in Mexico*.

The old University College, Nottingham (now the Public Library) which Lawrence attended.

Further reading

Editions of Lawrence's writings

A properly edited text of each of Lawrence's novels is now in preparation, to be published by Cambridge University Press. In the meantime, the best available texts are those in the Penguin series.

The Complete Poems have been splendidly edited in two volumes by Vivian de Sola Pinto and Warren Roberts (Heinemann, 1964).

The miscellaneous writings have been collected in two volumes, *Phoenix* I and II, also published by Heinemann (there is a selection made by A. A. H. Inglis in Penguins). The travel books and other discursive writings are also available in Penguins. *The Study of Thomas Hardy* and *Introduction to These Paintings* have been published by Heinemann in one paperback volume, edited by J. T. Davies.

The Collected Letters in eight volumes are being published by Cambridge University Press under the general editorship of Professor J. T. Boulton. Volume I appeared in 1979 and Volume II in 1982. There is also a volume of Letters edited with an introduction by Aldous Huxley (Heinemann, 1932) and two volumes edited by Harry T. Moore (Heinemann, 1962).

Bibliography

The standard bibliography is that by Warren Roberts in the Soho Bibliographies Series, *A Bibliography of D. H. Lawrence* (Hart-Davies, 1963)

Biography

The most comprehensive biography is undoubtedly the three-volume *D. H. Lawrence: A Composite Biography*, compiled, annotated and edited by Edward Nehls (Heinemann, 1957–9). This brings together in a fascinating and richly revealing way accounts of Lawrence by those who knew him at various periods of his life. Less voluminous but still very comprehensive is *The Priest of Love* by Harry T. Moore (rev. edn, Heinemann, 1974), an expanded version of the same author's earlier biography of Lawrence, *The Intelligent Heart*.

Nearly everybody who knew Lawrence felt impelled to write a book about him and some of them actually tell us something about Lawrence; Nehls has put the best parts of most of them in the Composite Biography.

General background

Two short books, both excellently illustrated, can be recommended:

MOORE, HARRY, T. and ROBERTS, WARREN: *D. H. Lawrence and His World* (Thames and Hudson).

SAGAR, KEITH: *The Life of D. H. Lawrence* (Eyre Methuen, 1980). There is also the fascinating and valuable memoir by Jessie Chambers ('E.T.'), *D. H. Lawrence: A Personal Record*, new edn with an introduction by J. D. Chambers (Jessie's brother) and other material (Frank Cass, 1965).

Criticism

There are literally hundreds of books on D. H. Lawrence and there is no sign of the number of volumes diminishing. The following is a drastically selective list:

CLARKE, COLIN: *River of Dissolution* (Routledge and Kegan Paul, 1969). A searching examination of *The Rainbow, Women in Love, The Plumed Serpent* and *Lady Chatterley's Lover* in relation to a central Romantic tradition.

DRAPER, R. P. (ed.) : *D. H. Lawrence: The Critical Heritage* (Routledge, 1970). A useful collection of early reviews of Lawrence with an introduction.

GILBERT, SANDRA: *Acts of Attention* (Cornell, 1972). A full-length study of the poetry.

GORDON, D. J.: *D. H. Lawrence as a Literary Critic* (Yale, 1966).

HOUGH, GRAHAM: *The Dark Sun* (Duckworth, 1956). A clear and helpful general survey of the work and the philosophy assumed to underlie it.

LEAVIS, F. R.: *D. H. Lawrence: Novelist* (Chatto and Windus, 1955). An influential book which has shaped much subsequent critical writing on Lawrence. Equally valuable is:

LEAVIS, F. R.: *Thought, Words and Creativity: Art and Thought in D. H. Lawrence* (Chatto and Windus, 1976).

MOYNAHAN, JULIAN: *The Deed of Life* (Princeton, 1963). A perceptive guide to the fiction.

OATES, JOYCE CAROL: *The Hostile Sun* (Black Sparrow Press, 1973). A short but stimulating pamphlet by the Canadian novelist.

SKLAR, SYLVIA: *The Plays of D. H. Lawrence* (Vision, 1975). A sympathetic study of Lawrence as a dramatist.

A selection of interesting essays on the novels mentioned will be found in *A Casebook on 'The Rainbow' and 'Women in Love'* edited by Colin Clarke and *A Casebook on 'Sons and Lovers'* edited by Gāmini Salgādo, both published by Macmillan, 1969. *The D. H. Lawrence Review* published by the University of Arkansas at Fayetteville has articles of critical, biographical, bibliographical and sometimes negligible interest. A useful guide to the Lawrence country is Bridget Pugh's *The Country of My Heart* published by Nottinghamshire County Library. There are extensive collections of Lawrence material at the University and City Libraries of Nottingham and at the Humanities Research Centre, University of Austin, Texas.

Index

General Index